Mediterranean Inspiration

125

HOME PLANS

INFLUENCED BY SOUTHERN EUROPEAN STYLE

Mediterranean Inspiration

Published by Home Planners, LLC
Wholly Owned by Hanley-Wood, LLC
One Thomas Circle, NW, Suite 600
Washington, DC 20005

Distribution Center
29333 Lorie Lane
Wixom, Michigan 48393

Group Vice President, General Manager, Andrew Schultz
Vice President, Publishing, Jennifer Pearce
Executive Editor, Linda Bellamy
Managing Editor, Jason D. Vaughan
Editor, Nate Ewell
Associate Editor, Simon Hyoun
Senior Plans Merchandiser, Morenci C. Clark
Plans Merchandiser, Nicole Phipps
Proofreader/Copywriter, Dyana Weis
Graphic Artist, Joong Min
Plan Data Team Leader, Ryan Emge
Production Manager, Brenda McClary

Vice President, Retail Sales, Scott Hill
National Sales Manager, Bruce Holmes
Director, Plan Products, Matt Higgins

For direct sales, contact Retail Vision at (800) 381-1288 ext 6053

BIG DESIGNS, INC.
President, Creative Director, Anthony D'Elia
Vice President, Business Manager, Megan D'Elia
Vice President, Design Director, Chris Bonavita
Editorial Director, John Roach
Assistant Editor, Tricia Starkey
Senior Art Director, Stephen Reinfurt
Production Director, David Barbella
Photo Editor, Christine DiVuolo
Art Director, Jessica Hagenbuch
Graphic Designer, Mary Ellen Mulshine
Graphic Designer, Lindsey O'Neill-Myers
Graphic Designer, Jacque Young
Assistant Photo Editor, Brian Wilson
Assistant Production Manager, Rich Fuentes

PHOTO CREDITS
Front Cover: Photo by Laurence Taylor
Back Cover: Photography by John Sciarrino, courtesy of Giovanni Photography

10 9 8 7 6 5 4 3 2 1

Printed in the United States of America

Library of Congress Catalog Control Number: 2004106198

ISBN: 1-931131-09-0

Veranda and terraced garden of a coastal home in Minorca, Spain.

Mediterranean Inspiration

Features

Home Plans

Ordering Information

Brightly colored tile roofs and whitewashed walls nearly outshine the sea and sky in San Vito Lo Capo, Sicily.

ABOVE: Gathered curtains bring a softening touch to the dramatically arched seating area of a public building. RIGHT: Recently caught and cleaned fish waiting for sale on the back of a truck at a local market.

Sea of Dreams

Few places on Earth move the imagination like the coastal lands of the Mediterranean. To follow the sun from the Aegean Sea, past Sicily, along the Italian Riviera and Côte d'Azur, to the Spanish coast and Morocco is to know how days can begin more slowly and linger like honey upon the cliffs and pebbled beaches. Once the confluence of ancient cultures such as the Romans, Moors, Ottomans, and Carthaginians, we love the Mediterranean for the graceful manner in which it cherishes its long history. And when we bring Mediterranean architecture home—in a row of slender columns or a pantiled *coppi* roof—we share in their common beauty. These details hold in place the timeless quality of our homes.

Mediterranean Inspiration begins by leading you on a tour of the region's architecture and design. Read about the area's rich and varied legacy and be inspired by the gallery of stunning Mediterranean-influenced homes. Proceed to our selection of home plans, starting with the "Featured Homes" on page 22 and continue to the showcase of homes ranging from under 2,500 square feet to over 3,500 square feet. When you find the plan that's right for you, turn to page 181 and begin fulfilling your dream of a Mediterranean retreat.

Mediterranean Architecture

With nature as its guide, the architecture of the Mediterranean offers a peaceful symmetry of organic and modern forms.

Traditional Mediterranean architecture reflects the priorities of life in a warm climate as well as the aesthetic sensibilities of its people. For instance, many traditional designs feature a central courtyard, both to cool the interior of the house and to create a natural environment in the heart of the home. Small windows hewn into exterior walls—often whitewashed and up to three-feet thick—help insulate rooms from the fiery sun and echo the regional preference for soft, naturalistic forms. Against this canvas, Mediterranean designers splash brightly painted doors, tiled mosaics, terra-cotta roofs, and other flourishes of saturated color.

Outside a country home in France, red flowers in window boxes and vines on the walls bring character and color to an otherwise unremarkable facade.

Mediterranean Architecture

Old World Mediterranean homes also reflect the regional economies. Wrought-iron gates and decorative hardware forged by local tradesmen make for rustic details around the home. Marble or other stones quarried nearby are used on surfaces and exteriors, carrying a common textural theme through the house. It is this preference for local materials that makes Mediterranean architecture so distinctively regional.

The designs featured in this book demonstrate how contemporary North American architects have cultivated Mediterranean themes in plans and details while retaining undeniably New World pleasures. For example, the centrality of the kitchen in the communal life of a home has been built into many of the book's featured designs. But gone are the low ceilings and molded-in surfaces, in favor of vertical freedom and clean lines. Also, the Mediterranean ethic of pampering visitors has been preserved in the accommodating guest rooms, often with private full baths. But what's good for the guest is even better for the owners, who will appreciate how well they can treat themselves in their truly gratifying master suite. Finally, many of the feature homes include an expansive rear lanai accompanying the courtyard and pool areas, which create spectacular outdoor spaces for quiet, casual use or entertaining. Protecting the space from the elements and unwanted visitors with an atrium enclosure will let you enjoy long, Mediterranean-inspired evenings with full peace of mind.

BELOW: Bright red flowers are colorful touches on this modest villa in Costa del Sol, Spain. LEFT: A more audacious iteration of Spanish forms is found in this home, plan HPT7600009 (page 33), which features a decorative chimney top and an impressive facade. The two-floor plan envisions a spacious family room and a lanai that spans the entire back of the home.

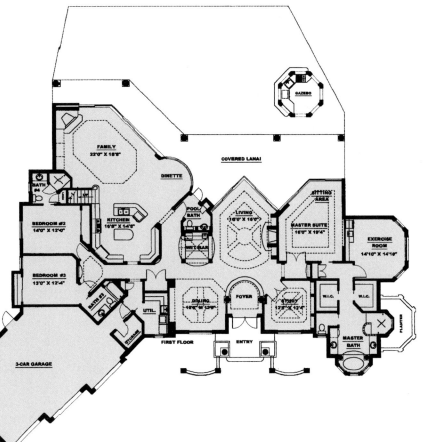

Mediterranean Architecture

SECOND FLOOR

FIRST FLOOR

ABOVE: Detail of a column that has taken on a rust-colored patina. **LEFT:** A hipped, tiled roof with brackets, trefoil window details, and an arched entry are undeniable Mediterranean features on this house, plan HPT7600017 (page 52). Note the large courtyard in the center of the design.

ABOVE: At a home in California, simple white columns and patterned tiles create a Moroccan-inspired seating area. **LEFT:** The dining room features a high ceiling, plant nook, and a large window to illuminate the space. From HPT7600009 (page 32).

Mediterranean Interiors

As in its architecture, Mediterranean design offers many surprising options for the homeowner. The following homes combine graceful tradition with exciting revisions.

Descriptions of traditional Mediterranean interiors often emphasize country aesthetics and overlook the decisive—but restrained—application of sophisticated designs and "modern" colors. Earth tones, patinaed materials, and distressed wood are commonly found in Mediterranean homes, but homeowners can also incorporate neon colors, refined tapestries, and "urban" furnishings. Decorative accents are an equally artful mix of antique and modern motifs.

Find your balance in the following photo gallery, which showcases the many contemporary expressions of Mediterranean design.

Opposite: The rustic mantle around the fireplace adds just the right weight of antiquity to this well-balanced representation of Mediterranean style. To see more of this home, proceed to plan HPT7600010 on page 45.

LEFT: Subtle geometric shapes in the curtains, doors, and floor tiles create a cool, tranquil sitting area in this Spanish villa. A space like this would be most welcome on days too hot for enjoying the courtyard. ABOVE: An unfussy garden requires only simple furnishings to become a charming sanctuary. Candles and lanterns could make the space perfect for entertaining at night.

OPPOSITE: Rustic furnishings like the basket-weave chairs and oversized clock balance homey comfort against the bare elegance of marble and of mirrored doors in this breakfast area. **LEFT:** Built-in shelves have been arched to match the large window in this study. Note the striped carpet and restrained use of animal print. Both rooms are from plan HPT7600009, page 33.

OPPOSITE: An arched niche lined with mosaic tiles encloses a cozy bath. Sculpted stone accents complete the scene. From plan HPT7600011, page 41. BELOW and LEFT: The tradition of the Mediterranean courtyard meets the radiance of modern materials in this spectacular indoor oasis. The nearby wet bar is a thoughtful accommodation.

Mediterranean Interiors

BELOW: Arched windows paired at a corner of the room allow for an expansive view of the yard. The headboard adds a smart Mediterranean flourish. See more of plan HPT7600012 on page 22. BELOW RIGHT: A pretty interior window between the breakfast nook and wet bar creates nested views of the many arched windows and niches in this home. From plan HPT7600010, page 45. RIGHT: A more traditional use of floor tiles and stucco, complete with a picturesque pair of wooden chairs. OPPOSITE: Bold use of antique furnishings and rich colors distinguish this bathroom. See plan HPT7600009, page 33.

Sicily in Style

What happens to a dream designed?
In this case, it shines even at night.

To the left of the entry, paired windows on a white wall effect a subtle but certain Mediterranean style to this grand design. The same appreciation for naturalistic forms can be seen in the rounded hallway from the main dining room to the nook and kitchen. A luxurious master suite occupies the left side of the plan, with private access to the covered patio. Guests will enjoy similar comforts in interestingly shaped rooms and full baths.

BELOW: Wide eaves and decorative molding complement a fine tile roof. RIGHT: A covered patio and porch overlooking the garden should make for picturesque and festive nights.

ABOVE: Bright whites against terra cotta tones suffuse drama in the dining room. RIGHT: A rounded vestibule echoes the whitewashed walls of eastern Mediterranean homes.

LEFT: A decorative backsplash adds a rustic touch to the gourmet island kitchen. BELOW: Tall niches accompanying a fireplace furnish a space for placed art and a pastoral fresco.

Feature Home

ABOVE: A built-in media center allows design themes to continue through the large family room. RIGHT: Arched windows paired at a corner allows for natural light throughout the day. The headboard adds a smart Mediterranean flourish.

The master
suite features a
tray ceiling and
private entrance
to the patio.

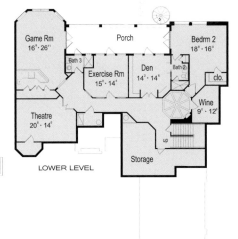

plan# HPT7600012

Style: Mediterranean
Main Level: 2,895 sq. ft.
Upper Level: 905 sq. ft.
Lower Level: 2,563 sq. ft.
Total: 6,363 sq. ft.
Bedrooms: 5
Bathrooms: 6½
Width: 73' - 4"
Depth: 89' - 0"
Foundation: Basement

SEARCH ONLINE @ EPLANS.COM

MAIN LEVEL

UPPER LEVEL

LOWER LEVEL

Bella Campania

A red tile roof and modest columns inflect Italian accents upon this contemporary design.

Softly angled turrets border this home's entryway, which opens into a spacious foyer, living room, and dining room area. Rounded arches gently mark the separation between rooms and preserve the plan's open spaces.

The house expresses in its indoor/outdoor relationships the spirit of Mediterranean living. A remarkable lanai nearly spans the rear of the plan. The space calls eagerly for a luxurious garden and pool, with views from the leisure room and the second-floor deck. A secluded master suite features a beautiful bay window, a coffered ceiling, and French doors to the lanai.

ABOVE: Bay windows and gorgeous roof lines make a dramatic curbside impression. OPPOSITE: A high, coffered ceiling and a view of the lanai bring even more breadth to this living room.

ABOVE: Large bay windows allow plenty of light for a seating area in the master suite. LEFT: Columns and arches provide a gentle transition from the foyer and living room to the dining room.

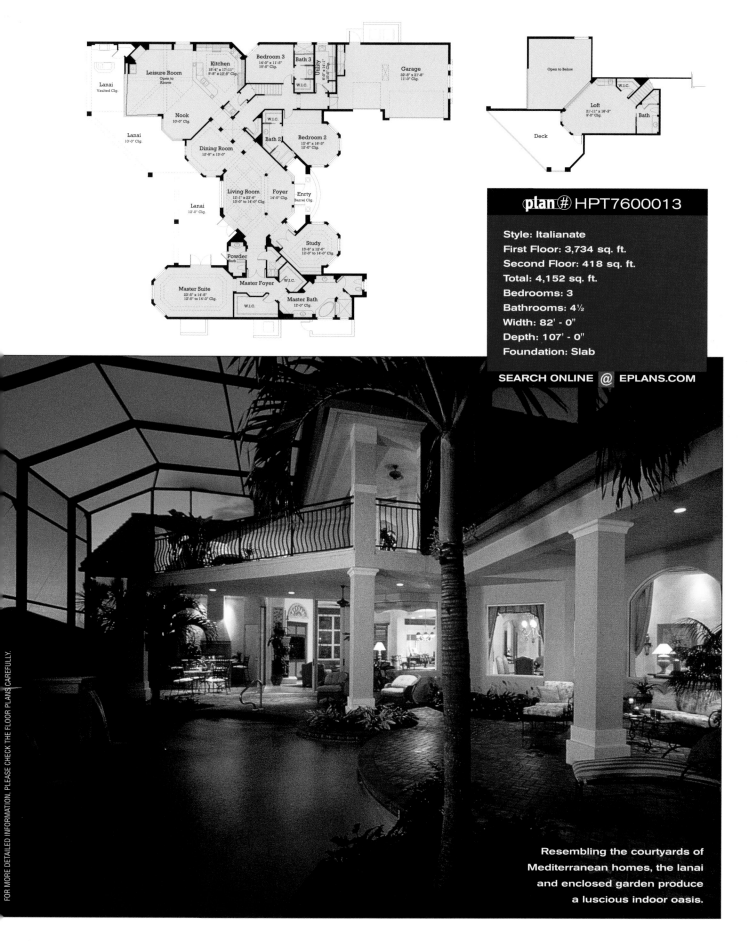

Lanai
Vaulted Clg.

Leisure Room
Open to
Above

Kitchen
15'-4" x 17'-11"
9'-8" x 10'-0" Clg.

Bedroom 3
14'-0" x 11'-5"
10'-0" Clg.

Bath 3

Utility

Garage
32'-8" x 31'-8"
11'-0" Clg.

Open to Below

W.I.C.

Loft
21'-11" x 16'-3"
9'-0" Clg.

Bath

Nook
10'-0" Clg.

Lanai
10'-0" Clg.

W.I.C.

Bedroom 2
12'-8" x 16'-3"
12'-0" Clg.

Dining Room
12'-8" x 13'-0"

Bath 2

Deck

Living Room
12'-1" x 23'-6"
13'-0" to 14'-0" Clg.

Foyer
14'-0" Clg.

Enrty
Barrel Clg.

Lanai
12'-0" Clg.

Study
15'-6" x 12'-6"
13'-0" to 14'-0" Clg.

Powder
Bath

Master Suite
23'-5" x 14'-8"
13'-0" to 14'-0" Clg.

Master Foyer

W.I.C.

W.I.C.

Master Bath
12'-0" Clg.

plan# HPT7600013

Style: Italianate
First Floor: 3,734 sq. ft.
Second Floor: 418 sq. ft.
Total: 4,152 sq. ft.
Bedrooms: 3
Bathrooms: 4½
Width: 82' - 0"
Depth: 107' - 0"
Foundation: Slab

SEARCH ONLINE @ EPLANS.COM

Resembling the courtyards of
Mediterranean homes, the lanai
and enclosed garden produce
a luscious indoor oasis.

Elegant Heights

*Grand details and a comfortable layout
make for easy elegance.*

Arched windows and a dramatic portico with scrolled columns are gracefully featured in this Mediterranean design. The foyer is just as expressive, with more scrolled columns and soft curves to match the arched doorway. Mosaic tiles on the floor and steps bring touches of color and polish to earth-toned surfaces. The master suite and bath with patio are to the right of the plan, while the guest rooms are to the left, near the family room and kitchen. A spacious lanai, here enclosed by a greenhouse, features a pool and spa lined with trees and other botanicals. Notice the wet bar, ready with cool drinks for visitors to this unexpected sanctuary.

ABOVE and OPPOSITE: A large fanlight over the door and matching windows complement the beautifully arched portico. Once inside, the same arches are echoed in the soft curves of the steps and scrolled columns.

PHOTOGRAPHY BY JOHN SCIARRINO, COURTESY OF GIOVANNI PHOTOGRAPHY

LEFT: Classical columns surround the bayed whirlpool bath. BELOW: Sliding glass doors and heavy curtains part to allow access from the master suite to the lanai. OPPOSITE: The spacious family room also opens onto the lanai.

FIRST FLOOR

SECOND FLOOR

plan# HPT7600009

Style: Mediterranean
First Floor: 3,633 sq. ft.
Second Floor: 695 sq. ft.
Total: 4,328 sq. ft.
Bedrooms: 5
Bathrooms: 5½
Width: 115' - 7"
Depth: 109' - 8"
Foundation: Slab

SEARCH ONLINE @ EPLANS.COM

Grand Entrance

This elegant Mediterranean home has everything you could hope for, from the unique living spaces to the glamorous master suite.

You'll love the way angled walls and open spaces work together in this contemporary design to create a warm and distinctive floor plan. A dual-facing fireplace in the middle of the house neatly separates the formal living room from the kitchen and large casual family room. Both spaces permit access to the covered patio in the rear, as does the master suite, which pushes the limits of luxury with double walk-in closets, bay windows, and an enormous bath with a corner windowed tub and separate vanities.

ABOVE: Just the right amount of landscaping complements the charming walkway and portico that greet visitors to this extraordinary home. OPPOSITE: The formal living room enjoys one side of the dual-facing fireplace.

The casual family room features a built-in media center and plenty of natural light.

Gentle arches and
classical columns
adorn the lanai.

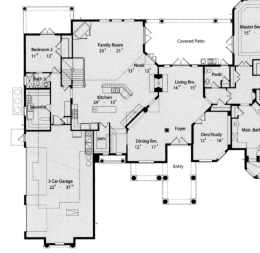

FIRST FLOOR

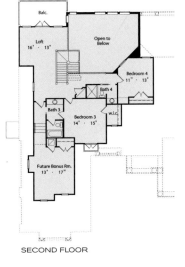

SECOND FLOOR

plan# HPT7600001

Style: Contemporary
First Floor: 3,478 sq. ft.
Second Floor: 1,037 sq. ft.
Total: 4,515 sq. ft.
Bonus Space: 314 sq. ft.
Bedrooms: 4
Bathrooms: 4½
Width: 86' - 8"
Depth: 84' - 4"
Foundation: Slab

SEARCH ONLINE @ EPLANS.COM

Perfect Manor

*Stunning Mediterranean style gives this home
a sense of palatial elegance.*

An arched portico and balustraded balcony are the centerpieces of the design's pleasingly symmetrical facade. Inside, a spectacular two-story foyer receives a sweeping staircase on the left that leads to a second-floor overlook connecting the left and right sides of the plan. This elevated space exhibits columns and soft arches, as well as cast-iron banisters of European fashion. Beyond the foyer, the dramatic height of the great room allows for more arches and pilasters on the walls.

ABOVE: Bracketed eaves and a near-flat roof are very faithful Italianate details. OPPOSITE: A remarkable foyer with sweeping staircase greets visitors in high style.

The family room flows
seamlessly into the
island kitchen, featuring
a rustic backsplash.

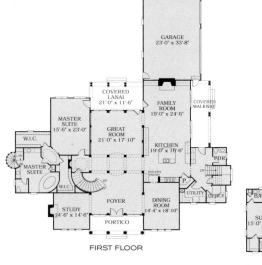

FIRST FLOOR

GARAGE
23'-0" x 33'-8"

COVERED
LANAI
21'-0" x 11'-6"

FAMILY
ROOM
19'-0" x 24'-6"

COVERED
WALKWAY

MASTER
SUITE
15'-6" x 23'-0"

GREAT
ROOM
21'-0" x 17'-10"

W.I.C.

KITCHEN
19'-0" x 16'-6"

MASTER
SUITE

PDR

W.I.C.

BUTLER'S
PANTRY

P.

UTILITY

OFFICE

STUDY
14'-6" x 14'-6"

FOYER

DINING
ROOM
14'-4" x 18'-10"

PORTICO

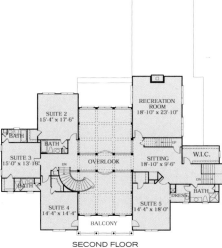

SECOND FLOOR

SUITE 2
15'-4" x 17'-6"

RECREATION
ROOM
18'-10" x 23'-10"

BATH

BATH

SUITE 3
15'-0" x 13'-10"

OVERLOOK

SITTING
18'-10" x 9'-6"

W.I.C.

BATH

DRESS

BATH

SUITE 4
14'-4" x 14'-4"

BALCONY

SUITE 5
14'-4" x 18'-0"

Cast-iron detailing on
the walls continues
the decorative theme
introduced in the foyer.

Cataluna Comfort

At over 7,000 square feet, this exuberant home with Spanish and Moroccan influences serves up generous helpings of Old World flavor.

An arched facade and delicately detailed colonnades welcome visitors to this inspired version of Mediterranean hauteur. Terra cotta tiles find great effect upon the hipped roof, especially atop the eight-sided conservatory and matching cupola. Again, the outdoor has been invited inside. The plan calls for an interior garden located centrally, near the kitchen, as well as a second, outdoor kitchen that opens into the veranda. Plus, the above-mentioned conservatory is a botanical oasis, placed only a few steps away from the master bedroom. The focal placement of the kitchen and the accompanying nook and leisure area reflect the Mediterranean ideal of cooking as a leisurely, familial affair.

Scrolled columns line the off-center porch of the home's gracefully embellished facade.

PHOTOGRAPHY BY LAURENCE TAYLOR

ABOVE: Owners have turned this conservatory into a dining area. Note how the rustic hearth and mantle balance the airy ceiling. OPPOSITE: Joining the leisure room and nook to the main kitchen draws guests and family to the life of the house.

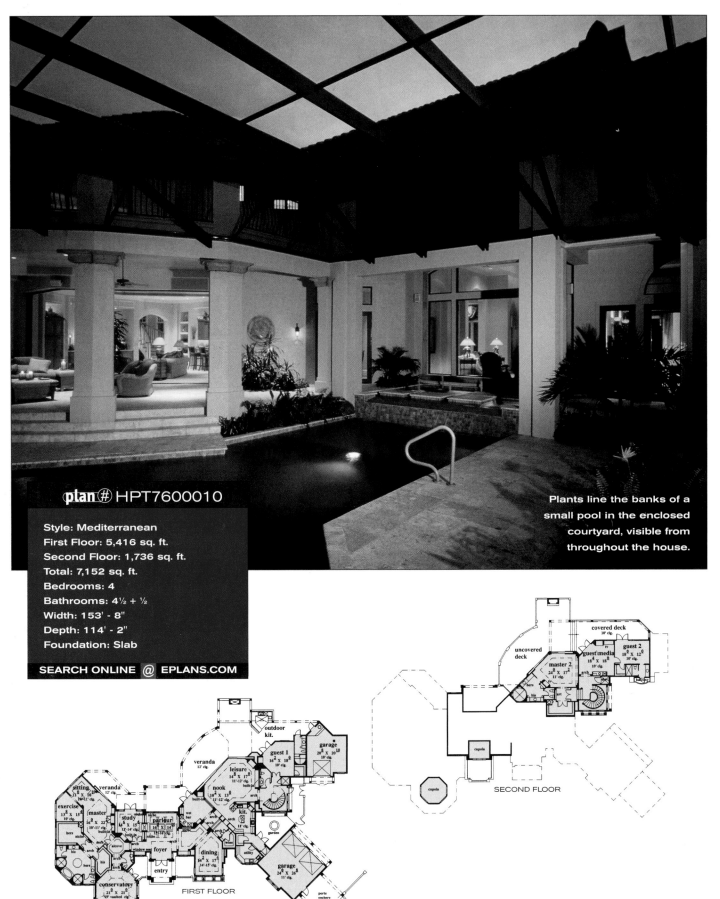

plan# HPT7600010

Style: Mediterranean
First Floor: 5,416 sq. ft.
Second Floor: 1,736 sq. ft.
Total: 7,152 sq. ft.
Bedrooms: 4
Bathrooms: 4½ + ½
Width: 153' - 8"
Depth: 114' - 2"
Foundation: Slab

SEARCH ONLINE @ EPLANS.COM

Plants line the banks of a small pool in the enclosed courtyard, visible from throughout the house.

FIRST FLOOR

SECOND FLOOR

THIS HOME, AS SHOWN IN THE PHOTOGRAPHS, MAY DIFFER FROM THE ACTUAL BLUEPRINTS.

Mediterranean Showcase

© Stephen Fuller, Inc.

B. DENT 04

Graced with beautiful details and gorgeous from any angle, this villa will charm all visitors. See more on page 57.

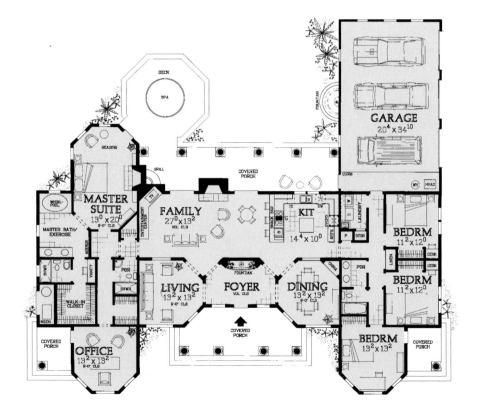

plan# HPT7600015

Style: Mediterranean
Square Footage: 2,831
Bedrooms: 4
Bathrooms: 3
Width: 84' - 0"
Depth: 77' - 0"
Foundation: Slab

SEARCH ONLINE @ EPLANS.COM

Besides great curb appeal, this home has a wonderful floor plan. The foyer features a fountain that greets visitors and leads to a formal dining room on the right and a living room on the left. A large family room at the rear has a built-in entertainment center and a fireplace. The U-shaped kitchen is perfectly located for servicing all living and dining areas. To the right of the plan, away from the central entertaining spaces, are three family bedrooms sharing a full bath. On the left side, with solitude and comfort for the master suite, are a large sitting area, an office, and an amenity-filled bath. A deck with a spa sits outside the master suite.

plan # HPT7600016

Style: Mediterranean
Square Footage: 2,987
Bedrooms: 3
Bathrooms: 3
Width: 74' - 4"
Depth: 82' - 4"
Foundation: Slab

SEARCH ONLINE @ EPLANS.COM

Classic columns, a tiled roof, and beautiful arched windows herald a gracious interior for this fine home. Arched windows also mark the entrance into the vaulted living room with a tiled fireplace. The dining room opens off the vaulted foyer. Filled with light from a wall of sliding glass doors, the family room leads to the covered patio—note the wet bar and range that enhance outdoor living. The kitchen features a vaulted ceiling and unfolds into the roomy nook, which boasts French doors to the patio. The master bedroom also has patio access and shares a dual fireplace with the master bath—a solarium lights this space. A vaulted study/den sits between two additional bedrooms.

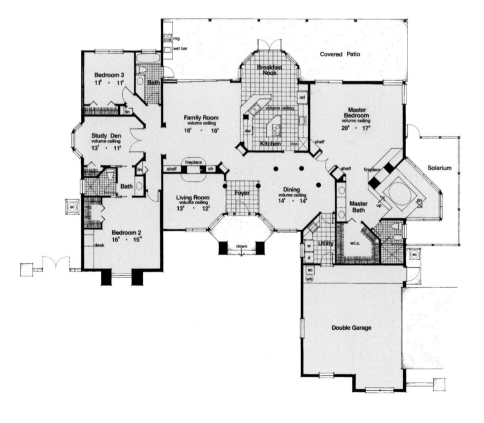

© The Sater Design Collection, Inc.

FIRST FLOOR

SECOND FLOOR

plan# HPT7600017

Style: Mediterranean
First Floor: 2,084 sq. ft.
Second Floor: 652 sq. ft.
Total: 2,736 sq. ft.
Bonus Space: 375 sq. ft.
Bedrooms: 3
Bathrooms: 2½
Width: 60' - 6"
Depth: 94' - 0"
Foundation: Slab

SEARCH ONLINE @ EPLANS.COM

With striking Mediterranean affluence, this renaissance estate invites family and guests with triplet arches and a dramatic vaulted portico. Upon entering, the bayed dining room is to the left; a study resides in the turret, bright with circumambient light courtesy of intricate full-length windows. The great room soars with a vintage exposed-beam ceiling and offers a fireplace and three sets of French doors to the veranda. Don't miss the country kitchen, a tribute to gourmet cooking. The master suite has an extended-bow window, access to the courtyard, and a luxurious bath with a Roman tub. An elegant staircase leads to two generous bedrooms; the vaulted bonus room is accessible from garage stairs or the outdoor deck off of Bedroom 3.

Mediterranean Showcase

© The Sater Design Collection, Inc.

plan# HPT7600018

Style: Italianate
Square Footage: 3,743
Bedrooms: 4
Bathrooms: 3½
Width: 80' - 0"
Depth: 103' - 8"
Foundation: Slab

SEARCH ONLINE @ EPLANS.COM

With California style and Mediterranean good looks, this striking stucco manor is sure to delight. The portico and foyer open to reveal a smart plan with convenience and flexibility in mind. The columned living room has a warming fireplace and access to the rear property. In the gourmet kitchen, an open design with an island and walk-in pantry will please any chef. From here, the elegant dining room and sunny nook are easily served. The leisure room is separated from the game room by a built-in entertainment center. The game area can also be finished off as a bedroom. To the rear, a guest room is perfect for frequent visitors or as an in-law suite. The master suite features a bright sitting area, oversized walk-in closets, and a pampering bath with a whirlpool tub. Extra features not to be missed: the outdoor grill, game-room storage, and gallery window seat.

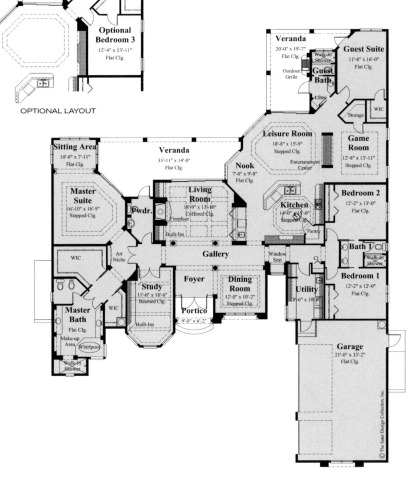

This home features two levels of pampering luxury filled with the most up-to-date amenities. Touches of Mediterranean detail add to the striking facade. A wrapping front porch welcomes you inside to a formal dining room and two-story great room warmed by a fireplace. Double doors from the master suite, great room, and breakfast nook access the rear veranda. The first-floor master suite enjoys a luxury bath, roomy walk-in closet, and close access to the front-facing office/study. Three additional bedrooms reside upstairs. The bonus room above the garage is great for an apartment or storage space.

plan# HPT7600019

Style: Mediterranean
First Floor: 2,219 sq. ft.
Second Floor: 1,085 sq. ft.
Total: 3,304 sq. ft.
Bonus Space: 404 sq. ft.
Bedrooms: 4
Bathrooms: 3½
Width: 91' - 0"
Depth: 52' - 8"
Foundation: Slab

SEARCH ONLINE @ EPLANS.COM

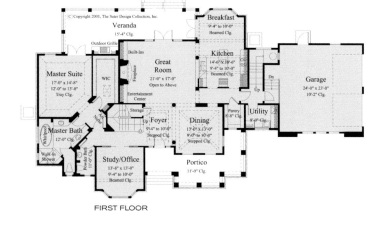

FIRST FLOOR

SECOND FLOOR

Mediterranean Showcase

© The Sater Design Collection, Inc.

plan# HPT7600020

Style: Mediterranean
First Floor: 3,025 sq. ft.
Second Floor: 1,639 sq. ft.
Total: 4,664 sq. ft.
Bonus Space: 294 sq. ft.
Bedrooms: 4
Bathrooms: 4½
Width: 70' - 0"
Depth: 100' - 0"
Foundation: Slab

SEARCH ONLINE @ EPLANS.COM

FIRST FLOOR

OPTIONAL LAYOUT

SECOND FLOOR

A Mediterranean masterpiece, this family-oriented design is ideal for entertaining. Double doors reveal a foyer, with a columned dining room to the right and a spiral staircase enclosed in a turret to the left. Ahead, the great room opens above to a soaring coffered ceiling. Here, a bowed window wall and a two-sided fireplace (shared with the study) make an elegant impression. The country-style kitchen is a host's dream, with an adjacent wet bar, preparation island, and space for a six-burner cooktop. Near the leisure room, a bayed nook could serve as a breakfast or reading area. The master suite is a pampering sanctuary, with no rooms directly above and personal touches you will surely appreciate. Upstairs, two bedrooms, one with a window seat, and a guest suite with a balcony, all enjoy private baths and walk-in closets.

Here is a Mediterranean classic complete with grand windows, columned entry and a balcony overhead. Windows wrap the home with sunshine. The bright floor plan includes a grand room—perfect for formal occasions—a family room featuring a fireplace—ideal for quality family time—and an expansive kitchen complete with a pantry and island. The master suite includes a sitting room with a ribbon of windows, two walk-in closets, dual vanities, and private access to the rear covered terrace. The second floor showcases three suites, each with their own baths, and an office.

plan # HPT7600021

Style: Mediterranean
Main Level: 3,300 sq. ft.
Upper Level: 1,974 sq. ft.
Lower Level: 1,896 sq. ft.
Total: 7,170 sq. ft.
Bedrooms: 5
Bathrooms: 4½
Width: 108' - 2"
Depth: 74' - 7"
Foundation: Basement

SEARCH ONLINE @ EPLANS.COM

LOWER LEVEL

MAIN LEVEL

UPPER LEVEL

© Stephen Fuller, Inc.

plan# HPT7600022

Style: Mediterranean
First Floor: 1,900 sq. ft.
Second Floor: 1,676 sq. ft.
Total: 3,576 sq. ft.
Bedrooms: 3
Bathrooms: 3½
Width: 67' - 0"
Depth: 82' - 6"
Foundation: Crawlspace

SEARCH ONLINE @ EPLANS.COM

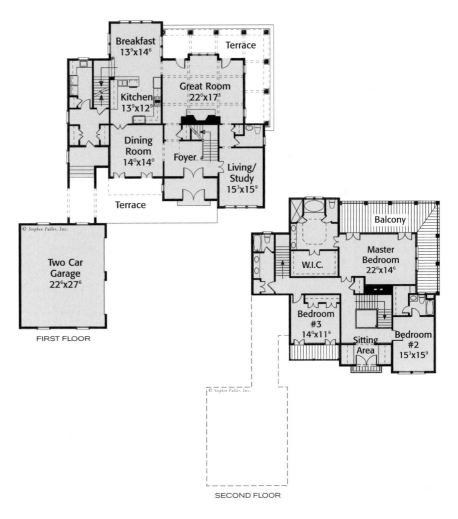

Absolutely gorgeous from any angle, this Mediterranean villa will delight and inspire. Enter off the front terrace to the formal foyer; the living room (or study) opens on the right through French doors. The nearby dining room is graced with French doors that lead out to the terrace and bring fresh air in. Abundant counter space in the kitchen makes it simple to serve the adjoining breakfast nook. The great room hosts an enchanting beamed ceiling, large, warming fireplace, and access to the rear terrace. Upstairs, two bedrooms, each with their own baths, share a sitting area and lovely balcony. A lavish bath and wrapping balcony mark the master suite and make this retreat as a true haven.

© The Sater Design Collection, Inc.

plan# HPT7600023

Style: Italianate
Square Footage: 2,191
Bedrooms: 3
Bathrooms: 2½
Width: 62' - 10"
Depth: 73' - 6"
Foundation: Slab

SEARCH ONLINE @ EPLANS.COM

Perfect for a corner lot, this Mediterranean villa is a beautiful addition to any neighborhood. Low and unassuming on the outside, this plan brings modern amenities and classic stylings together for a great family home. The study and two-story dining room border the foyer; an elongated gallery introduces the great room. Here, a rustic beamed ceiling, fireplace, and art niche are thoughtful touches. The step-saving U-shaped kitchen flows into a sunny bayed breakfast nook. To the far right, two bedrooms share a full bath. The master suite is separated for privacy, situated to the far left. French-door access to the veranda and a sumptuous bath make this a pleasurable retreat.

Mediterranean Showcase

© The Sater Design Collection, Inc.

plan # HPT7600024

Style: Mediterranean
Square Footage: 3,640
Bedrooms: 3
Bathrooms: 3½
Width: 106' - 4"
Depth: 102' - 4"
Foundation: Slab

SEARCH ONLINE @ EPLANS.COM

Come home to luxurious living—all on one level—with this striking Mediterranean plan. Unique ceiling treatments highlight the living areas—the living and dining rooms, as well as the study, feature stepped ceilings, and the leisure room soars with a vaulted ceiling. The gourmet kitchen includes a spacious center island; another kitchen, this one outdoors, can be accessed from the leisure room. The master suite boasts plenty of amenities: a large, skylit walk-in closet, a bath with a whirlpool tub and walk-in shower, and private access to a charming garden area. Two suites, both with private baths, sit to the right of the plan.

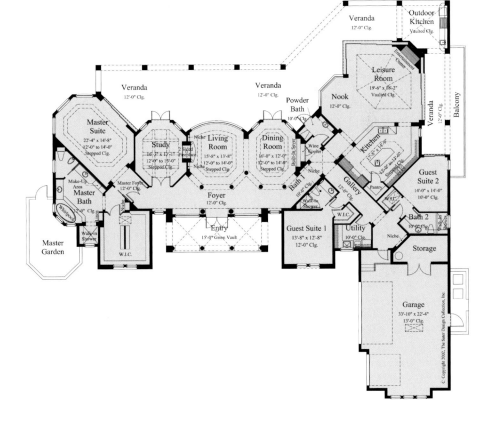

Giving the impression of a luxurious villa resort, this Italian Country home is a study in fine living. Arched windows mark the grand entry, where a formal foyer reveals an elegant dining room on the right and a light-filled great room just ahead. Three family suites are located on the left, graced by a curved-window hallway. The master suite enjoys solitude on the upper level and hosts a private sitting room and lavish bath with a separate vanity and Roman tub. Other extras not to be missed: a cabana bath, eight pairs of French doors to the rear lanai, and ample garage storage.

plan# HPT7600025

Style: Italianate
First Floor: 3,745 sq. ft.
Second Floor: 1,250 sq. ft.
Total: 4,995 sq. ft.
Bedrooms: 4
Bathrooms: 4½
Width: 95' - 4"
Depth: 89' - 10"
Foundation: Slab

SEARCH ONLINE @ EPLANS.COM

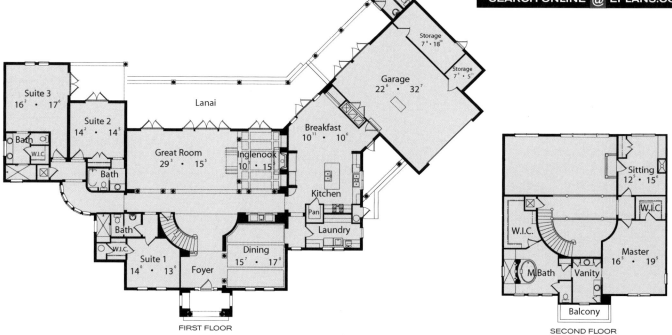

FIRST FLOOR

SECOND FLOOR

Mediterranean Showcase

plan# HPT7600026

Style: Italianate
First Floor: 2,567 sq. ft.
Second Floor: 844 sq. ft.
Total: 3,411 sq. ft.
Bonus Space: 297 sq. ft.
Bedrooms: 4
Bathrooms: 3½ + ½
Width: 56' - 8"
Depth: 85' - 4"
Foundation: Slab

SEARCH ONLINE @ EPLANS.COM

For serene beauty, both inside and out, this two-story Italianate home can't be beat. The elegant front entry and the covered rear patio call out for the right combination of flowers and shrubs to enhance the home's graceful exterior features. Downstairs, the master suite gloriously offers twin walk-in closets and vanities, a gigantic tub, and a separate shower; upstairs, three bedrooms share two baths and a computer room. The living areas on the first level are designed for full comfort and ease for a busy family and for formal get-togethers. A good-sized laundry room and a two-car garage with the option of building a room above it complete this plan.

SECOND FLOOR

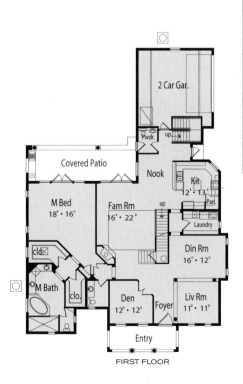

FIRST FLOOR

This Italian Renaissance marvel has it all—five bedrooms, a game room, a theater, and expansive areas for formal parties and relaxed barbecues. A covered patio winds around the entire rear of the home, and a sundeck is located on the second level. A wet bar and circular balcony, with an outside spiral stairway, make the upstairs game room a great party site. The lavish master suite features a circular sitting area with windows drawing in natural light from many directions. A spiral stairway winds gracefully upstairs from the impressive main-floor entry, or, if you prefer, take the elevator. A semicircular turret on the corner of the three-car garage is not only flashy, it is a handy storage area.

plan# HPT7600004

Style: Mediterranean
First Floor: 4,323 sq. ft.
Second Floor: 2,226 sq. ft.
Total: 6,549 sq. ft.
Bonus Space: 453 sq. ft.
Bedrooms: 5
Bathrooms: 5½ + ½
Width: 98' - 8"
Depth: 102' - 8"
Foundation: Slab

SEARCH ONLINE @ EPLANS.COM

FIRST FLOOR

SECOND FLOOR

plan # HPT7600003

Style: Mediterranean
First Floor: 2,926 sq. ft.
Second Floor: 1,268 sq. ft.
Total: 4,194 sq. ft.
Bonus Space: 353 sq. ft.
Bedrooms: 4
Bathrooms: 4½
Width: 75' - 0"
Depth: 85' - 4"
Foundation: Slab

SEARCH ONLINE @ EPLANS.COM

This magnificent Mediterranean-style home is full of the charms that make entertaining gracious and family life comfortable. From the elegant covered entry, pass into the foyer or, through separate French doors, into the den on the right and the formal dining room on the left. A superb kitchen, sunlit breakfast nook, and family room flow together, creating a relaxed unit. Splendor awaits in the master suite with its gracefully curved bedchamber, huge walk-in wardrobes, and luxuriant bath. On the opposite side of the house, a guest bedroom enjoys a full bath. Two more bedrooms share a bath on the second level, and additional space is available for another bedroom and bath. The rear covered patio can be entered from the living room, the master suite, or the breakfast nook. Three vehicles will easily fit into the side-loading garage.

© The Sater Design Collection, Inc.

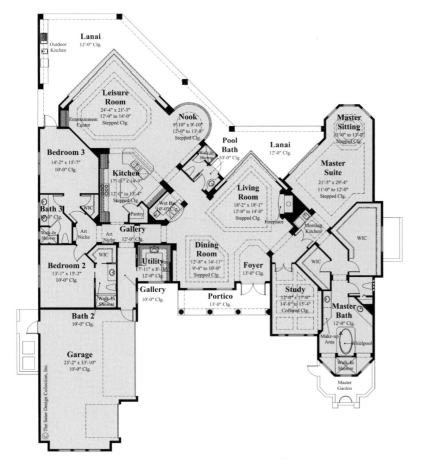

plan# HPT7600027

Style: Italianate
Square Footage: 3,942
Bedrooms: 3
Bathrooms: 4
Width: 83' - 10"
Depth: 106' - 0"
Foundation: Slab

SEARCH ONLINE @ EPLANS.COM

Italian Renaissance flair sets the tone for this majestic Old World estate. An impressive entrance reveals an open floor plan; the foyer, living room and dining room are all defined by distinctive ceiling treatments for endless interior design possibilities. A wet bar and pool bath announce the gourmet kitchen with a pentagonal island and lots of counter space. Past a half-moon nook, the leisure room will be a family favorite. On the lanai, an outdoor kitchen is an easy way to cook up all-weather fun. To the far right, the master suite will amaze; an octagonal sitting area and morning kitchen are only the beginning. Two enormous walk-in closets beckon with built-in shelving and room for even the biggest clotheshorse collections. The master bath, set in a turret, will soothe and pamper with a central whirlpool tub, walk-in shower, and views to the garden.

Seaside Escapes

A Mediterranean vacation home is the perfect blend of refinement and relaxation. See more on page 97.

A soaring arched entry and a stucco exterior establish this design's strong Mediterranean influences. Inside, the living room adjoins the kitchen and dinette area. Three bedrooms cluster to the right of the plan—the master bedroom boasts a walk-in closet and a full bath, and the two additional bedrooms share a full hall bath.

plan# HPT7600029

Style: Mediterranean
Square Footage: 1,742
Bedrooms: 3
Bathrooms: 2
Width: 62' - 0"
Depth: 43' - 0"
Foundation: Basement

SEARCH ONLINE @ EPLANS.COM

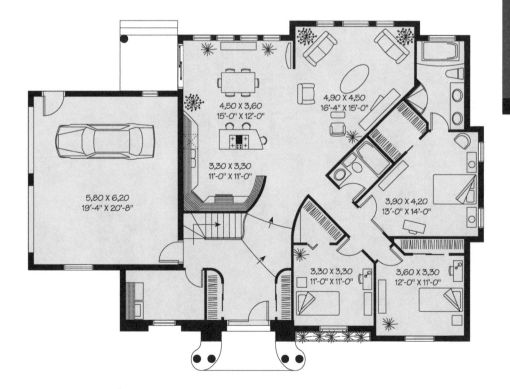

ORDER BLUEPRINTS 24 HOURS, 7 DAYS A WEEK, AT 1-800-521-6797

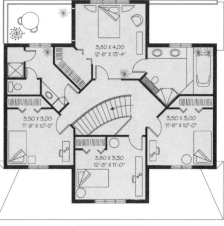

plan# HPT7600030

Style: Mediterranean
First Floor: 1,065 sq. ft.
Second Floor: 1,032 sq. ft.
Total: 2,097 sq. ft.
Bedrooms: 4
Bathrooms: 2½
Width: 38' - 0"
Depth: 38' - 0"
Foundation: Basement

SEARCH ONLINE @ EPLANS.COM

This Mediterranean home offers a dreamy living-by-the-water lifestyle, but it's ready to build in any region. A lovely arch-top entry announces an exquisite foyer with a curved staircase. The family room provides a fireplace and opens to the outdoors on both sides of the plan. An L-shaped kitchen serves a cozy morning area as well as a stunning formal dining room, which offers a bay window. Second-floor sleeping quarters include four bedrooms and two bathrooms. The master suite opens to a balcony and offers a bath with a double-bowl vanity.

SECOND FLOOR

FIRST FLOOR

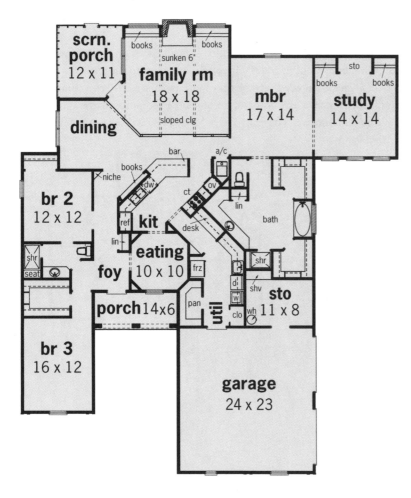

plan # HPT7600031

Style: Mediterranean
Square Footage: 2,349
Bedrooms: 3
Bathrooms: 2
Width: 63' - 0"
Depth: 74' - 0"
Foundation: Crawlspace, Slab

SEARCH ONLINE @ EPLANS.COM

This stunning Sun Country design offers a convenient arrangement of rooms all on one level. Inside, the kitchen with a serving bar offers easy access to the casual eating room and the dining room. Two family bedrooms are located to the left and share a hall bath. The master bedroom enjoys a spacious bath with twin walk-in closets and a private study with built-in bookshelves. A sloped ceiling shapes the cozy family room warmed by a fireplace, with flanking bookshelves. The rear screened porch is a brisk retreat. The utility room leads to the two-car garage with storage.

ORDER BLUEPRINTS 24 HOURS, 7 DAYS A WEEK, AT 1-800-521-6797

© 91 HOME DESIGN SERVICES, INC.

plan # HPT7600007

Style: Mediterranean
Square Footage: 1,550
Bedrooms: 3
Bathrooms: 2
Width: 43' - 0"
Depth: 59' - 0"
Foundation: Slab

SEARCH ONLINE @ EPLANS.COM

Enjoy resort-style living in this striking Mediterranean home. Guests will always feel welcome when entertained in the formal living and dining areas, but the eat-in country kitchen overlooking the family room will be the center of attention. Enjoy casual living in the large family room and out on the patio with the help of an optional summer kitchen and a view of the fairway. Built-in shelves and an optional media center provide decorating options. The master suite features a volume ceiling and a spacious master bath.

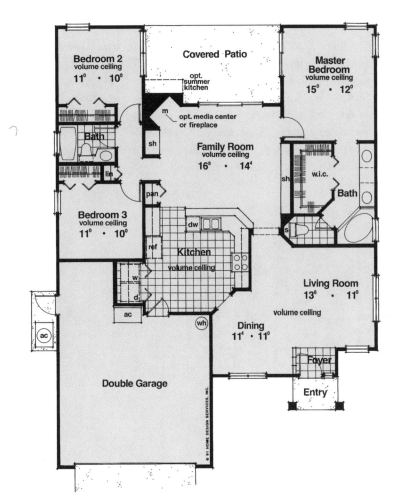

With its elegant hipped rooflines, stucco-and-stone detailing, arched windows, and gabled roofs, this home presents its European heritage with pride. The covered entryway leads to a formal dining room defined by graceful columns and arched openings. Columns and arched openings also lead into the vaulted great room, where a welcoming fireplace waits to warm cool evenings, and radius windows flood the room with light. The kitchen is sure to please with its angled counter and accessibility to the bayed breakfast nook. Two family bedrooms are to the right of the design. The master suite is to the left, a modern split design that belies the Old World flavor evident in this home.

plan # HPT7600032

Style: Mediterranean
Square Footage: 2,188
Bonus Space: 674 sq. ft.
Bedrooms: 3
Bathrooms: 2½
Width: 58' - 0"
Depth: 64' - 4"
Foundation: Crawlspace, Slab, Basement

SEARCH ONLINE @ EPLANS.COM

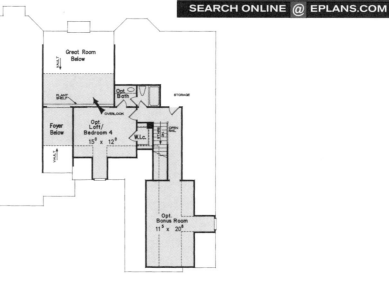

ORDER BLUEPRINTS 24 HOURS, 7 DAYS A WEEK, AT 1-800-521-6797

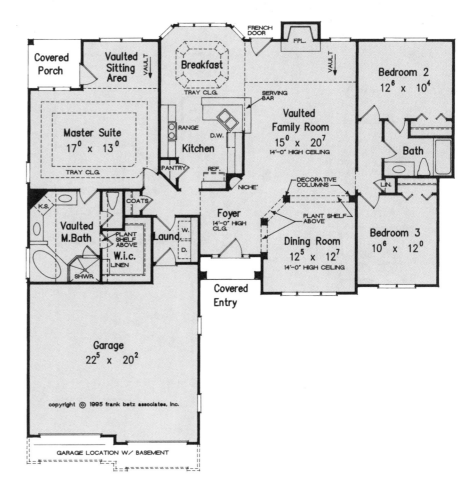

plan# HPT7600033

Style: Mediterranean
Square Footage: 1,779
Bedrooms: 3
Bathrooms: 2
Width: 57' - 0"
Depth: 56' - 4"
Foundation: Basement, Crawlspace

SEARCH ONLINE @ EPLANS.COM

European style shines from this home's facade in the form of its stucco detailing, hipped rooflines, fancy windows, and elegant entryway. Inside, decorative columns and a plant shelf define the formal dining room, which works well with the vaulted family room. The efficient kitchen offers a serving bar to both the family room and the deluxe breakfast room. Located apart from the family bedrooms for privacy, the master suite is sure to please with its many amenities, including a vaulted sitting area and a private covered porch. The two secondary bedrooms share a full hall bath.

Seaside Escapes

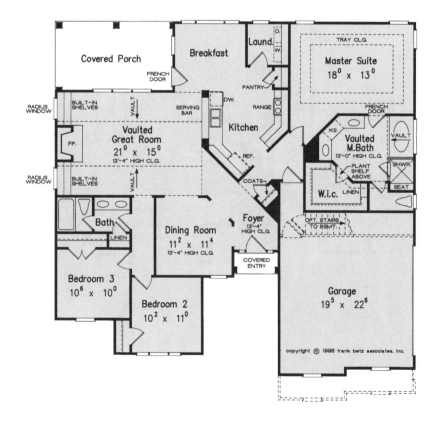

plan# HPT7600034

Style: Mediterranean
Square Footage: 1,756
Bedrooms: 3
Bathrooms: 2
Width: 52' - 6"
Depth: 51' - 6"
Foundation: Crawlspace, Basement

SEARCH ONLINE @ EPLANS.COM

This sweet ranch-style home uses chic ceiling treatments to adorn its creative floor plan. With lots of focal-point wallspace, this home is perfect for the aspiring art collector—or artist! The angled foyer directs you to the vaulted great room, where built-in bookshelves and an extended-hearth fireplace enjoy natural light through radius windows. Toward the front of the home reside two family bedrooms. In the opposite corner, the master suite revels in privacy and grandeur.

plan# HPT7600035

Style: Mediterranean
Square Footage: 2,479
Bedrooms: 3
Bathrooms: 2½
Width: 73' - 0"
Depth: 75' - 6"
Foundation: Crawlspace, Basement

SEARCH ONLINE @ EPLANS.COM

Mediterranean features and delicate window treatments set this home apart from the crowd. The kitchen is really the showpiece of this home. Opening up to the breakfast area and family room, a cooktop island, generous room to move and tons of counter and cabinet space will make this a favorite gathering place. The vaulted family room can be a multimedia entertainment center or a quiet place to read and relax. With a floor plan designed for families, all of the sleeping areas are in the right wing. The massive master suite will delight with a spectacular bath and a charming sitting nook.

FIRST FLOOR

SECOND FLOOR

Asymmetrical gables, pediments, and tall, arch-top windows accent a European-style exterior; inside, an unrestrained floor plan expresses its independence. A spider-beam ceiling and a centered fireplace framed by shelves redraw the open space of the family room to cozy dimensions. The vaulted breakfast nook enjoys a radius window and a French door that leads outside. Split sleeping quarters lend privacy to the luxurious master suite.

plan# HPT7600036

Style: French Country
Square Footage: 2,403
Bonus Space: 285 sq. ft.
Bedrooms: 3
Bathrooms: 2½
Width: 60' - 0"
Depth: 67' - 0"
Foundation: Crawlspace,
Basement, Slab

SEARCH ONLINE @ EPLANS.COM

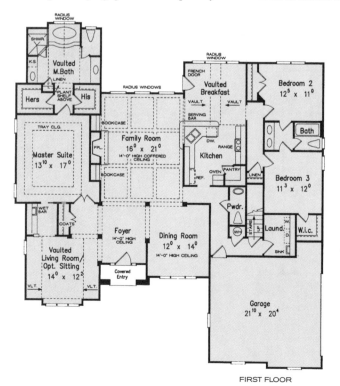

FIRST FLOOR

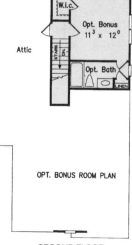

OPT. BONUS ROOM PLAN

SECOND FLOOR

ORDER BLUEPRINTS 24 HOURS, 7 DAYS A WEEK, AT 1-800-521-6797

plan⊕ HPT7600037

Style: Mediterranean
Square Footage: 2,201
Bedrooms: 3
Bathrooms: 2½
Width: 59' - 6"
Depth: 62' - 0"
Foundation: Crawlspace, Basement

SEARCH ONLINE @ EPLANS.COM

Contemporary accents and captivating interior spaces dazzle this perfect family floor plan. The spacious foyer is flanked on either side by formal living and dining rooms. Beyond, the vaulted family room offers a spacious casual area warmed by a fireplace. The kitchen opens to the vaulted breakfast nook. The luxurious master suite features His and Hers walk-in closets and a vaulted bath with an enticing whirlpool tub. Two additional family bedrooms offer access to a Jack-and-Jill bath. A laundry room connects to the two-car garage.

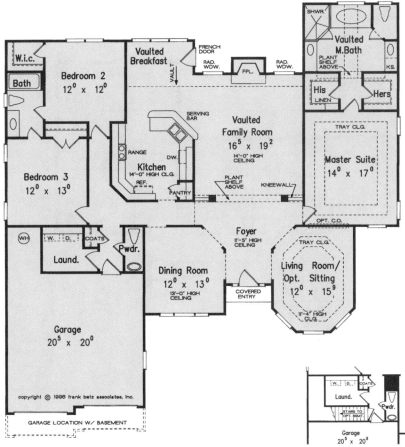

Seaside Escapes

plan # HPT7600038

Style: Mediterranean
Square Footage: 1,503
Bedrooms: 3
Bathrooms: 1
Width: 59' - 8"
Depth: 44' - 4"
Foundation: Basement

SEARCH ONLINE @ EPLANS.COM

Traditional lines and an elegant double-door entry give this contemporary home curb appeal. In front, a large picture window is accented by a slight arch and keystone. The living room—just to the left of the foyer—is open to the dining room, which features a bumped-out bay flooding the area with natural light and ambience. The L-shaped kitchen boasts an island and serves the dining and living rooms with ease. Two family bedrooms are down the hall. The master suite enjoys plenty of closet space, and the spacious full bath features a separate tub and shower.

ORDER BLUEPRINTS 24 HOURS, 7 DAYS A WEEK, AT 1-800-521-6797

© 2000 Donald A. Gardner, Inc.

plan # HPT7600039

Style: Mediterranean
Square Footage: 1,707
Bedrooms: 3
Bathrooms: 2
Width: 56' - 6"
Depth: 45' - 8"

SEARCH ONLINE @ EPLANS.COM

Mediterranean and French influences brighten this country home, which offers a covered front porch and a deck in the rear. The foyer opens to the great room, with marvelous views, and the formal dining room. The angled kitchen adjoins the breakfast nook. Two family bedrooms sit at the front sharing a full bath. The master suite, with a large walk-in closet and private bath, is tucked behind the garage for privacy.

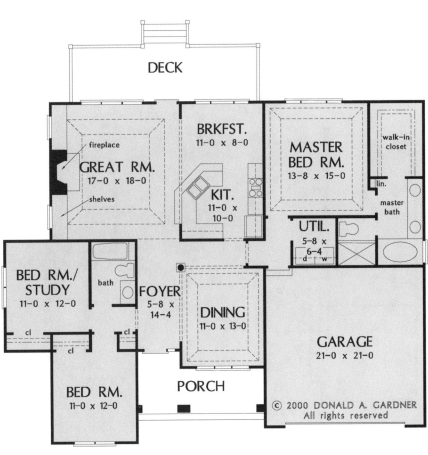

© 2000 Donald A. Gardner, Inc.

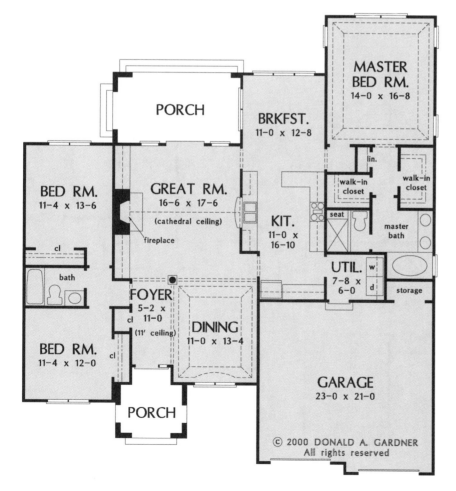

PORCH

MASTER BED RM.
14-0 x 16-8

BRKFST.
11-0 x 12-8

BED RM.
11-4 x 13-6

GREAT RM.
16-6 x 17-6
(cathedral ceiling)

fireplace

KIT.
11-0 x
16-10

lin.

walk-in closet

walk-in closet

seat

master bath

cl

bath

FOYER
5-2 x
11-0
(11' ceiling)

cl

DINING
11-0 x 13-4

UTIL.
7-8 x
6-0

w
d

storage

BED RM.
11-4 x 12-0

cl

PORCH

GARAGE
23-0 x 21-0

plan# HPT7600040

Style: Mediterranean
Square Footage: 1,831
Bedrooms: 3
Bathrooms: 2
Width: 54' - 6"
Depth: 60' - 6"

SEARCH ONLINE @ EPLANS.COM

This one-story, three-bedroom design takes its inspiration from the French and Neo-French Eclectic periods, with the steeply pitched hipped roof and the entry's elevated arch. Very modern in design, the interior boasts an efficient arrangement of private and social areas. The hub of social activities is definitely the great room, which adjoins the dining room, opens to the rear porch, and enjoys a pass-through to the kitchen. Tray ceilings grace the formal dining room and the master suite that includes two walk-in closets, double-sink vanity, tub, and compartmented shower and toilet.

ORDER BLUEPRINTS 24 HOURS, 7 DAYS A WEEK, AT 1-800-521-6797

© 2000 Donald A. Gardner, Inc.

plan# HPT7600041

Style: Mediterranean
Square Footage: 2,098
Bedrooms: 3
Bathrooms: 2
Width: 60' - 0"
Depth: 63' - 8"

SEARCH ONLINE @ EPLANS.COM

This three-bedroom home fits nicely into any neighborhood, with its complex hipped roof and stucco facade offering a European/Mediterranean flair. The vaulted great room, with a fireplace, built-ins, and a window wall that opens to the covered porch, adjoins the elegant dining room where decorative columns and a tray ceiling set a formal tone. The rear porch can be accessed as well by the breakfast nook, which enjoys a sunny location abutting the kitchen, and the master bedroom.

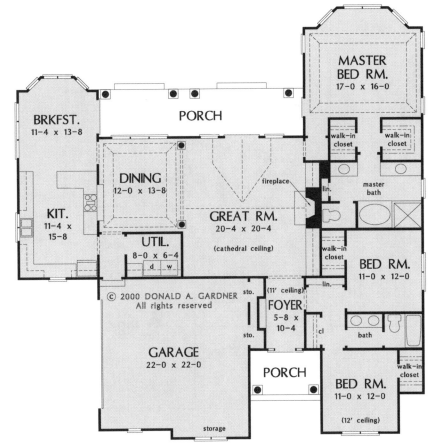

plan# HPT7600042

Style: Mediterranean
Square Footage: 1,970
Bedrooms: 3
Bathrooms: 2
Width: 57' - 8"
Depth: 58' - 0"

SEARCH ONLINE @ EPLANS.COM

Perfect proportions and attention to detail make this Mediterranean home one in a million. Enter from the courtyards to the tiled foyer and continue to the massive great room. A two-way fireplace shares its glow with the hearth room. The well-planned kitchen enjoys light from a rear bay and sliding glass doors and easily serves the intricately adorned dining room. Two bedrooms (or make one a den) share a skylit bath on the far left. The master suite provides privacy and relishes a lovely ceiling treatment, skylit whirlpool bath, and access to the rear courtyard, which accommodates a soothing hot tub.

plan # HPT7600043

Style: Mediterranean
Square Footage: 1,954
Bedrooms: 4
Bathrooms: 2½
Width: 64' - 10"
Depth: 58' - 10"

SEARCH ONLINE @ EPLANS.COM

Direct from the Mediterranean, this Spanish-style, one-story home offers a practical floor plan. The facade features arch-top, multipane windows; a columned front porch; a tall chimney; and a tiled roof. The interior has a wealth of livability. What you'll appreciate first is the juxtaposition of the great room and the formal dining room—both defined by columns. A more casual eating area is attached to the L-shaped kitchen and accesses a screened porch, as does the great room. Three bedrooms mean abundant sleeping space. The study could be a fourth bedroom—choose the full bath option in this case. A tray ceiling decorates the master suite, which is further enhanced by a bath with a separate shower and tub, walk-in closet, and double sinks.

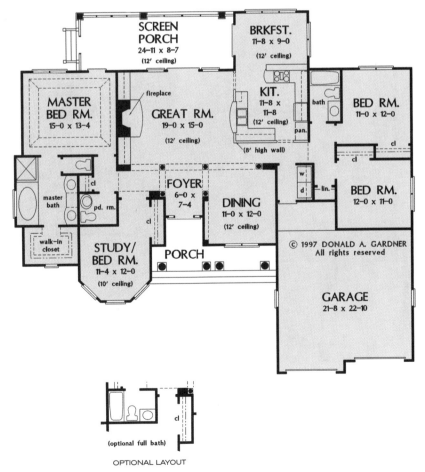

(optional full bath)

OPTIONAL LAYOUT

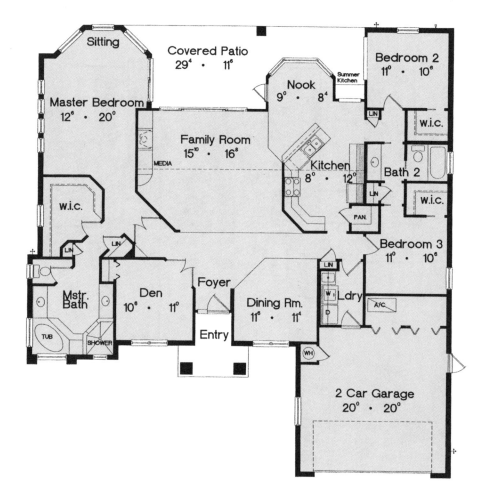

plan # HPT7600044

Style: Mediterranean
Square Footage: 2,118
Bedrooms: 3
Bathrooms: 2
Width: 58' - 0"
Depth: 62' - 0"
Foundation: Slab

SEARCH ONLINE @ EPLANS.COM

The lavishness of the exterior of this home is continued inside, culminating with the expansive master suite. A wall of windows, a sitting area with a bay window, and a luxuriant bath with a garden tub combine to create a pampering suite. The large family room enjoys a built-in media center and double sets of sliding glass doors that open to the covered patio. The well-equipped kitchen is situated conveniently between the formal dining room and the sunny breakfast nook.

ORDER BLUEPRINTS 24 HOURS, 7 DAYS A WEEK, AT 1-800-521-6797

plan# HPT7600045

Style: Mediterranean
Square Footage: 1,717
Bedrooms: 3
Bathrooms: 2
Width: 58' - 0"
Depth: 62' - 0"
Foundation: Basement

SEARCH ONLINE @ EPLANS.COM

A triplet of keystone arches mimicking recessed fan-light windows hints at the elegance to be found within this charming European-style home. Stucco and stone and classical porch columns highlight the beauty of the exterior. Vast amenities await within this compact one-story design. Inside, columns define the formal dining and great rooms. Both the great room and the master suite boast French doors that open to the expansive veranda with its optional outdoor kitchen—perfect for summer afternoons. An alluring fireplace warms the great room. Space is masterfully used in the master suite with its walk-in closet, double-sink vanity, separate shower, tub, and compartmented bath. The left side of the plan holds two family bedrooms that share a full bath, a utility room, and the two-car garage. Both of the family bedrooms also provide walk-in closets. Don't miss the sunny nook overlooking the veranda and the well-equipped kitchen with a walk-in pantry.

plan# HPT7600046

Style: Mediterranean
Square Footage: 2,397
Bedrooms: 3
Bathrooms: 2½
Width: 73' - 2"
Depth: 73' - 2"
Foundation: Slab

SEARCH ONLINE @ EPLANS.COM

Dramatic rooflines and a unique entrance set the mood of this contemporary home. Double doors lead into the foyer, which opens directly to the formal living and dining rooms. A den/study is adjacent to this area and offers a quiet retreat. The spacious kitchen features a large cooktop work island and plenty of counter and cabinet space. The spacious family room expands this area and features a wall of windows and a warming fireplace. Two secondary bedrooms share a full bath. The master suite is designed with pleasure in mind. Included in the suite are a lavish bath and a deluxe walk-in closet, as well as access to the covered patio.

Seaside Escapes

plan# HPT7600047

Style: Mediterranean
First Floor: 1,352 sq. ft.
Second Floor: 1,000 sq. ft.
Total: 2,352 sq. ft.
Bedrooms: 4
Bathrooms: 3
Width: 52' - 0"
Depth: 55' - 0"
Foundation: Slab

SEARCH ONLINE @ EPLANS.COM

A covered patio shades the entry to the foyer of this home—it is lit by an arched window. Double doors to the right open to a guest room with an arched picture window. The great room, open to the level above, has a wet bar; a large rear patio also offers a wet bar. The tiled kitchen provides a serving bar for the breakfast room. French doors in the master bedroom open onto a deck. The spacious bath here includes a walk-in closet, twin vanities, and spa tub. Two additional bedrooms and a bath complete the second level. The front bedroom includes a study and opens onto a deck. The plan can be built with a flat-tiled or barrel roof.

FIRST FLOOR

SECOND FLOOR

plan# HPT7600048

Style: Mediterranean
Square Footage: 2,221
Bedrooms: 4
Bathrooms: 3
Width: 65' - 0"
Depth: 50' - 0"
Foundation: Slab

SEARCH ONLINE @ EPLANS.COM

The raised foyer and living room bring an interesting change of levels to this ingenious plan. The family room, with a 12-foot wall of sliding glass doors, brings the outside in, and the entertainment/fireplace wall wows visitors. The efficient kitchen features a pantry and easy access to the sunny breakfast nook. Three secondary bedrooms are conveniently separated from the master suite. The rear bedroom doubles as a guest or in-law suite and shares the pool bath. The open and airy master suite, located off the nook, accesses the patio. The master bath holds a corner soaking tub, an oversized shower, a large double vanity with a make-up area, and double walk-in closets.

ORDER BLUEPRINTS 24 HOURS, 7 DAYS A WEEK, AT 1-800-521-6797

Seaside Escapes

© The Sater Design Collection, Inc.

plan # HPT7600049

Style: Spanish
Square Footage: 2,194
Bedrooms: 3
Bathrooms: 2½
Width: 62' - 10"
Depth: 73' - 6"
Foundation: Slab

SEARCH ONLINE @ EPLANS.COM

A squared portico and stone accents lend European charm to any neighborhood. Intriguing and unique, this beautiful chateau would look great from the California coast to the farmlands of New Hampshire. Inside, 10-foot ceilings with distinctive treatments set the tone for luxury. The great room is the heart of the home, offering cozy nights by the fireplace and sunny days through a triplet of French doors to the veranda. The kitchen is designed for efficiency and elegance, with an island and a bayed breakfast nook. Split-bedroom planning situates two bedrooms to the right; the master suite resides on the far left. Here, a pampering bath and veranda access are a welcome indulgence.

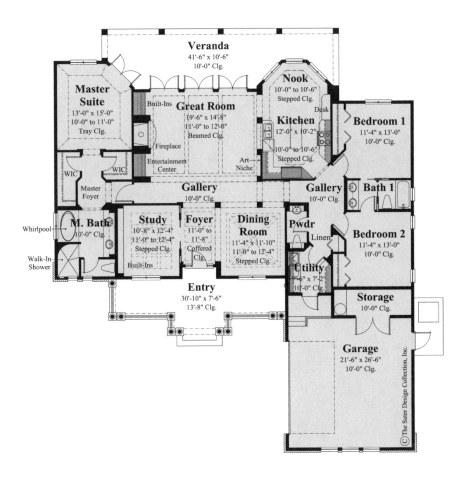

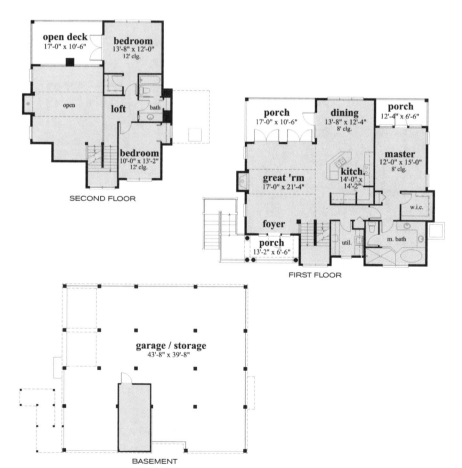

open deck
17'-0" x 10'-6"

bedroom
13'-8" x 12'-0"
12' clg.

open

loft

bath

bedroom
10'-0" x 13'-2"
12' clg.

SECOND FLOOR

porch
17'-0" x 10'-6"

dining
13'-8" x 12'-4"
8' clg.

porch
12'-4" x 6'-6"

great 'rm
17'-0" x 21'-4"

kitch.
14'-0" x
14'-2"

master
12'-0" x 15'-0"
8' clg.

w.i.c.

foyer

porch
13'-2" x 6'-6"

util.

m. bath

FIRST FLOOR

garage / storage
43'-8" x 39'-8"

BASEMENT

plan # HPT7600050

Style: Italianate
First Floor: 1,342 sq. ft.
Second Floor: 511 sq. ft.
Total: 1,853 sq. ft.
Bedrooms: 3
Bathrooms: 2
Width: 44' - 0"
Depth: 40' - 0"
Foundation: Basement

SEARCH ONLINE @ EPLANS.COM

Historic architectural details and timeless materials come together in this outrageously beautiful home. With a perfect Mediterranean spirit, arch-top windows create curb appeal and allow the beauty and warmth of nature within. To the rear of the plan, an elegant dining room easily flexes to serve traditional events as well as impromptu gatherings. An angled island counter accents the gourmet kitchen and permits wide interior vistas. The master bedroom features a spacious bedroom that leads outside to a private porch. On the upper level, an open deck extends the square footage of one of the secondary bedrooms.

plan # HPT7600051

Style: Mediterranean
First Floor: 1,492 sq. ft.
Second Floor: 854 sq. ft.
Total: 2,346 sq. ft.
Bonus Space: 810 sq. ft.
Bedrooms: 3
Bathrooms: 3½
Width: 44' - 0"
Depth: 48' - 0"
Foundation: Basement

SEARCH ONLINE @ EPLANS.COM

This lovely pier home is the picture of island living. Space on the lower level is devoted to the garage, but allows for a storage area if needed. The first floor holds the great room, with access to a rear porch. The dining room and kitchen are nearby for easy access. The master suite is also on this floor and features porch access and a stunning bath. Two family bedrooms with private baths and a loft area are found on the second floor. A porch can be accessed from each of the bedrooms.

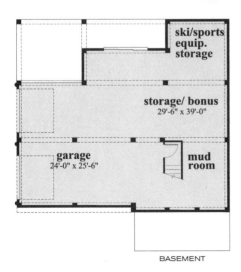

BASEMENT

FIRST FLOOR

SECOND FLOOR

This enticing European villa boasts an Italian charm and a distinct Mediterranean feel. The foyer steps lead up to the formal living areas. To the left, a study is expanded by a vaulted ceiling and double doors that open to the front balcony. The island kitchen is conveniently open to a breakfast nook. The guest quarters reside on the right side of the plan—one suite boasts a private bath; the other uses a full hall bath. The secluded master suite features two walk-in closets and a pampering whirlpool master bath. The home is completed by a basement-level garage.

plan # HPT7600052

Style: Italianate
Square Footage: 2,385
Bedrooms: 3
Bathrooms: 3
Width: 60' - 0"
Depth: 52' - 0"
Foundation: Slab

SEARCH ONLINE @ EPLANS.COM

ORDER BLUEPRINTS 24 HOURS, 7 DAYS A WEEK, AT 1-800-521-6797

plan# HPT7600053

Style: Italianate
First Floor: 1,143 sq. ft.
Second Floor: 651 sq. ft.
Total: 1,794 sq. ft.
Bonus Space: 476 sq. ft.
Bedrooms: 2
Bathrooms: 2½
Width: 32' - 0"
Depth: 57' - 0"
Foundation: Slab

SEARCH ONLINE @ EPLANS.COM

Italian Country elegance graces the exterior of this casa bellisima, swept in Mediterranean enchantment. The covered entryway extends into the foyer, where straight ahead, the two-story great room spaciously enhances the interior. This room features a warming fireplace and offers built-in cabinetry. The open dining room extends through double doors to the veranda on the left side of the plan. The adjacent kitchen features efficient pantry space. A family bedroom with a bath, a powder room, and a utility room also reside on this main floor. Upstairs, a vaulted master suite with a vaulted private bath and deck share the floor with a loft area, which overlooks the great room. Downstairs, the basement-level bonus room and storage area share space with the two-car garage. Two lanais open on either side of the bonus room for additional outdoor patio space.

FIRST FLOOR

BASEMENT

SECOND FLOOR

The mixture of grand details with a comfortable layout makes this home a perfect combination of elegance and easy living. Those who prefer a spacious master suite set apart from the rest of the home will love this arrangement. The top story is devoted to a master suite with double doors leading to a private porch and a loft that overlooks the vaulted great room below. On the first floor, each of the two family bedrooms has an adjoining porch. The built-ins and fireplace in the great room give a feeling of casual sophistication.

plan# HPT7600054

Style: Mediterranean
First Floor: 1,383 sq. ft.
Second Floor: 595 sq. ft.
Total: 1,978 sq. ft.
Bonus Space: 617 sq. ft.
Bedrooms: 3
Bathrooms: 2
Width: 48' - 0"
Depth: 42' - 0"
Foundation: Basement

SEARCH ONLINE @ EPLANS.COM

BASEMENT

FIRST FLOOR

SECOND FLOOR

ORDER BLUEPRINTS 24 HOURS, 7 DAYS A WEEK, AT 1-800-521-6797

plan # HPT7600055

Style: Mediterranean
First Floor: 874 sq. ft.
Second Floor: 880 sq. ft.
Total: 1,754 sq. ft.
Bedrooms: 3
Bathrooms: 2½
Width: 34' - 0"
Depth: 43' - 0"
Foundation: Basement

SEARCH ONLINE @ EPLANS.COM

A stately tower adds a sense of grandeur to contemporary high-pitched rooflines on this dreamy Mediterranean-style villa. Surrounded by outdoor views, the living space extends to a veranda through three sets of French doors. Decorative columns announce the dining area, which boasts a 10-foot ceiling and views of its own. Tall arch-top windows bathe a winding staircase with sunlight or moonlight. The upper-level sleeping quarters include a master retreat that offers a bedroom with views and access to the observation deck. Secondary bedrooms share a full bath and linen storage. Bedroom 3 features a walk-in closet and French doors to the deck.

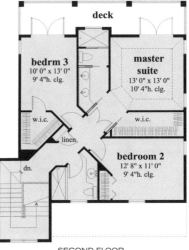

SECOND FLOOR

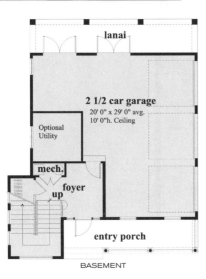

BASEMENT

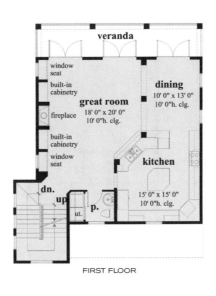

FIRST FLOOR

Decorative window ornaments, hipped rooflines, and second-floor flower boxes give this two-story European-style home a touch of elegance. A lavish bath on the upper level serves three comfortable bedrooms with ample closet space; a linen closet is off the hallway. The dining area and living room are open to each other, creating considerable flexibility for arranging furniture. The well-equipped kitchen serves the dining room at one end, and a peninsular snack counter at the other end will be a favorite spot for quick breakfasts and late-night munching. A walk-in shower is available in the first-floor bath, as well as a washer and dryer.

plan # HPT7600056

Style: Mediterranean
First Floor: 689 sq. ft.
Second Floor: 676 sq. ft.
Total: 1,365 sq. ft.
Bedrooms: 3
Bathrooms: 2
Width: 26' - 0"
Depth: 26' - 4"
Foundation: Basement

SEARCH ONLINE @ EPLANS.COM

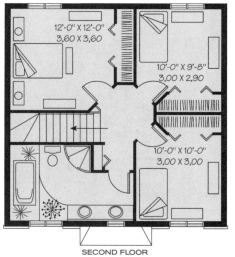

14'-0" X 12'-4"
4,20 X 3,70

10'-8" X 10'-0"
3,20 X 3,00

8'-0" X 14'-4"
2,40 X 4,30

FIRST FLOOR

12'-0" X 12'-0"
3,60 X 3,60

10'-0" X 9'-8"
3,00 X 2,90

10'-0" X 10'-0"
3,00 X 3,00

SECOND FLOOR

ORDER BLUEPRINTS 24 HOURS, 7 DAYS A WEEK, AT 1-800-521-6797

plan# HPT7600057

Style: French
First Floor: 825 sq. ft.
Second Floor: 825 sq. ft.
Total: 1,650 sq. ft.
Bedrooms: 3
Bathrooms: 2
Width: 30' - 0"
Depth: 28' - 0"
Foundation: Basement

SEARCH ONLINE @ EPLANS.COM

The stately aura of this rustic European-style home, enhanced by the stone exterior, introduces an interior that is both comfortable and convenient. The family cooks will appreciate the thought that has gone into designing a kitchen that has more than adequate counter and cabinet space and easy access to the living room via the snack bar. A gas fireplace warms the living room. A downstairs bathroom with a shower has enough room for the washer and dryer. Three second-floor bedrooms share a deluxe bath with a corner garden tub, shower, and double-sink vanity. An alcove at the end of the hall is lighted by a circular window and can serve as a modest sitting area.

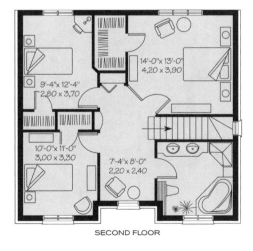

SECOND FLOOR

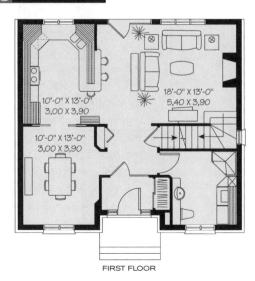

FIRST FLOOR

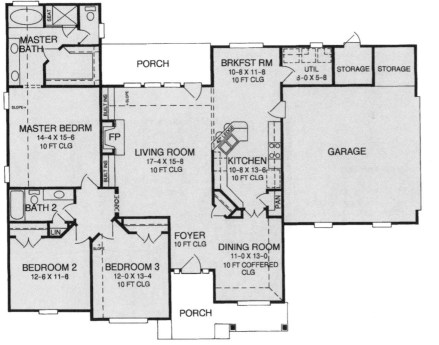

This charming cottage home possesses a heart of gold with French folk style. An arched stone entrance welcomes you inside beyond the front porch. Wide views invite natural light and provide a sense of spaciousness in the living room. A fireplace with an extended hearth is framed by built-in bookcases and complemented by a sloped ceiling. A well-organized kitchen provides wrapping counters and a serving ledge, which overlooks the breakfast area. The formal dining room is highlighted by a coffered ceiling and enjoys easy service from the kitchen. The master suite features a private bath with a garden tub and a separate shower with a seat. Two additional family bedrooms share a full hall bath.

ORDER BLUEPRINTS 24 HOURS, 7 DAYS A WEEK, AT 1-800-521-6797

Inviting Villas

A French-inspired villa on a country landscape is always a pleasure. See more on page 125.

Inviting Villas

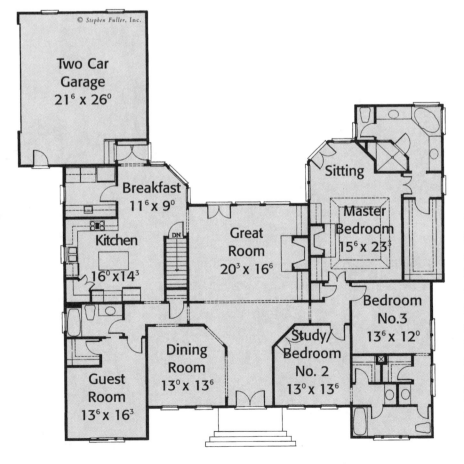

plan # HPT7600060

Style: Mediterranean
Square Footage: 2,785
Bedrooms: 4
Bathrooms: 3
Width: 72' - 0"
Depth: 72' - 0"
Foundation: Walkout Basement

SEARCH ONLINE @ EPLANS.COM

This elegant design boasts many Mediterranean influences such as the stucco facade, corner quoins, and arched windows. The foyer is flanked by a formal dining room and a study, which converts to an additional bedroom. Straight ahead, the great room, featuring a fireplace and built-ins, accesses the rear yard. The island kitchen opens to a breakfast nook for casual occasions. The master suite on the opposite side of the home boasts wondrous amenities such as a private fireplace, a bayed sitting area accessing the rear, a lavish bath, and an enormous walk-in closet.

plan# HPT7600061

Style: French
Square Footage: 2,713
Bedrooms: 3
Bathrooms: 2½
Width: 94' - 0"
Depth: 62' - 0"
Foundation: Slab

SEARCH ONLINE @ EPLANS.COM

Intriguing rooflines, lovely window treatments, and a stately brick facade will bring European elegance to any neighborhood. A four-way vault ceiling in the living room and dining room (and Bedroom 2) are beautiful touches; built-in bookshelves and a corner fireplace will make the living room the heart of the home. A flexible floor plan allows the kitchen's serving bar to access the eating area, or use the space as a den and enjoy all your meals in the dining room. The master bedroom features chamfer corners and a luxurious private bath.

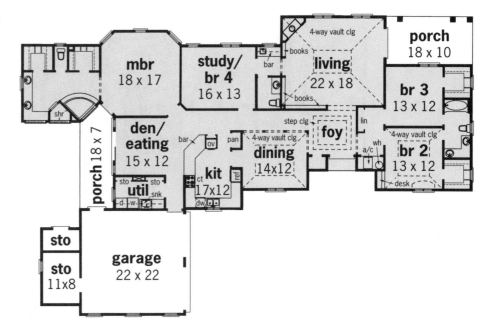

Master
Bedroom
14'4"x 18'4"

Covered Porch
21'5"x 10'6"

Walk-In
Closet

Walk-In
Closet

Master
Bath

Bath

Foyer

Bedroom
11'10"x 13'

Porch

Living
21'6"x 23'

Dining
14'5"x 14'

Breakfast
14'x 11'4"

Kitchen
14'x 13'

Utility

Bedroom
12'6"x 11'6"

Bath

Dressing

Bedroom
12'x 12'

Two Car
Garage
21'2"x 26'

Unfinished
Gameroom
11'4"x 26'

plan# HPT7600062

Style: Mediterranean
Square Footage: 2,781
Bonus: 319 sq. ft.
Bedrooms: 4
Bathrooms: 3
Width: 64' - 10"
Depth: 76' - 9"
Foundation: Slab, Crawlspace

SEARCH ONLINE @ EPLANS.COM

A multifaceted facade and classic arches blend with
an intricate hipped roof design, dressing this home
with a sheer sense of elegance. The dining and
living rooms meld with the breakfast nook creating
an expansive common area that spills out onto the
rear covered porch. The four bedrooms are split
with two on each side of the plan—the master suite
on the left boasts a lavish master bath and twin
walk-in closets. The unfinished game room easily
converts to a home office or attic storage.

ORDER BLUEPRINTS 24 HOURS, 7 DAYS A WEEK, AT 1-800-521-6797

plan# HPT7600063

Style: Mediterranean
Square Footage: 2,558
Bedrooms: 4
Bathrooms: 3
Width: 63' - 6"
Depth: 71' - 6"
Foundation: Basement

SEARCH ONLINE @ EPLANS.COM

Heavy corner quoins make a rustic impression that is dressed up by a subtly asymmetrical design and arches on the windows. The centerpiece of the home is a magnificent family room with a tray ceiling, fireplace, built-in shelves, and access to the rear covered porch. Adjacent, the breakfast room connects to the kitchen, which serves the formal dining room through elegant double doors. Two secondary bedrooms secluded on the far right of the plan each provide private access to a full bath with twin vanities. To the far left are a third bedroom and the spacious master suite, which features His and Hers walk-in closets, an oval tub, separate shower, compartmented toilet, and twin vanities.

plan# HPT7600064

Style: Mediterranean
Square Footage: 2,660
Bedrooms: 4
Bathrooms: 3
Width: 66' - 4"
Depth: 74' - 4"
Foundation: Slab

SEARCH ONLINE @ EPLANS.COM

Circle-top windows are beautifully showcased in this magnificent home. The double-door entry leads into the foyer and welcomes guests into a formal living and dining room area with wonderful views. As you approach the entrance to the master suite, you pass the den/study, which can easily become a guest or bedroom suite. A gently bowed soffit and stepped ceiling treatments add excitement to the master bedroom, with floor-length windows framing the bed. The bay-window sitting area further enhances the opulence of the suite. The master bath comes complete with a double vanity, a make-up area, and a soaking tub balanced by the large shower and private toilet chamber. The walk-in closet caps off this well-appointed space with ample hanging and built-in areas.

ORDER BLUEPRINTS 24 HOURS, 7 DAYS A WEEK, AT 1-800-521-6797

plan# HPT7600065

Style: Mediterranean
Square Footage: 2,539
Bedrooms: 3
Bathrooms: 2½
Width: 75' - 2"
Depth: 68' - 8"
Foundation: Slab

SEARCH ONLINE @ EPLANS.COM

Enjoy this beautiful home, complete with Spanish influences! Exposed rafter tails, arched porch detailing, massive paneled front doors, and stucco exterior walls enhance the Western character of this U-shaped ranch house. Double doors open to a spacious, slope-ceilinged art gallery. The quiet sleeping zone is comprised of an entire wing. The extra room at the front of this wing may be used for a den or an office. The family dining and kitchen activities are located at the opposite end of the plan. Indoor-outdoor living relationships are outstanding. The large, open courtyard is akin to the fabled Greek atrium. It is accessible from each of the zones and functions with a covered arbor, which looks out over the rear landscape. The master suite has a generous sitting area, a walk-in closet, twin lavatories, a whirlpool tub, and a stall shower.

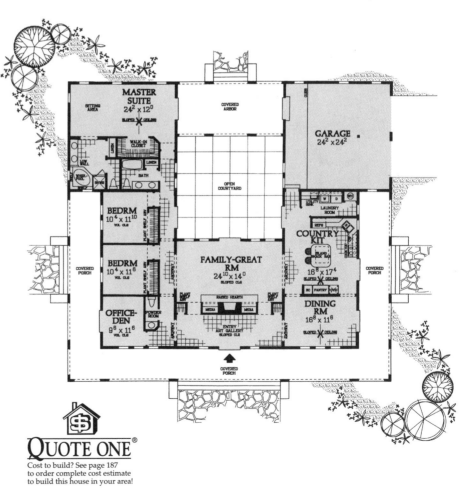

QUOTE ONE®
Cost to build? See page 187
to order complete cost estimate
to build this house in your area!

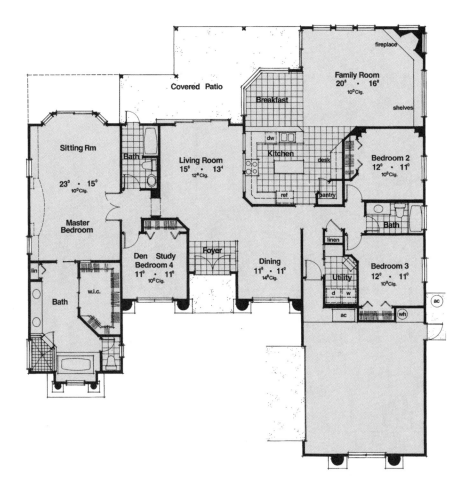

plan# HPT7600066

Style: Mediterranean
Square Footage: 2,743
Bedrooms: 4
Bathrooms: 3
Width: 67' - 0"
Depth: 75' - 0"
Foundation: Slab

SEARCH ONLINE @ EPLANS.COM

Monumental arches grace this classic facade allowing light to spill into the spacious interior of this four-bedroom home. The dining room sits to the right of the foyer, open to the living room and conveniently near the kitchen. Two family bedrooms share a full bath and convenient access to the garage at the right of the design. The kitchen, breakfast nook, and family room feature an open layout. The U-shaped kitchen enjoys a serving bar, walk-in pantry, built-in desk, and rectangular island work area. Enjoy plenty of evenings at home in this beautiful family room with its corner fireplace, built-in shelves, and lovely views of the backyard.

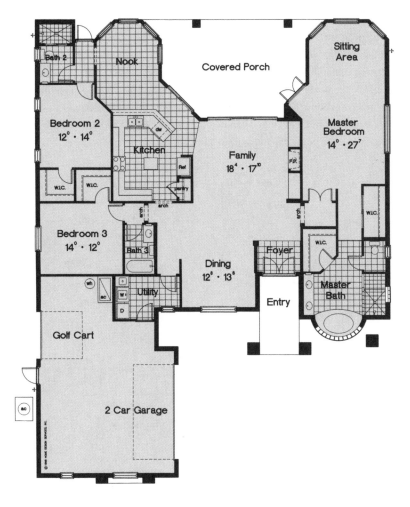

plan # HPT7600067

Style: Italianate
Square Footage: 2,503
Bedrooms: 3
Bathrooms: 3
Width: 60' - 0"
Depth: 78' - 4"
Foundation: Slab

SEARCH ONLINE @ EPLANS.COM

Square pillars elegantly introduce the entry of this gracious three-bedroom home. Past the two-door entry, a Mediterranean-style family room impresses guests. The built-in entertainment center surrounding the fireplace enhances the spacious feel of the living room. To the right resides a master suite with a sunny sitting area, two walk-in closets, private access to the rear covered porch, and a master bath featuring a soaking tub set in a concave wall of glass. To the left of the design are the two family bedrooms—note the walk-in closets and private baths for each room—a kitchen, bayed breakfast nook, and handy utility room. This home would be perfect for placement on or near a golf course—the plan includes its own golf-cart garage door.

This magnificent villa boasts a beautiful stucco exterior framing a spectacular entry. The heart of the home is served by a well-crafted kitchen with wrapping counter space and an island cooktop counter. The breakfast nook enjoys a view of the veranda and beyond, and brings natural light to the casual eating space. Archways supported by columns separate the dining room from the great room, which boasts a fireplace and built-in cabinetry. On the upper level, the master suite features a sitting area and a private veranda. The master bath provides a kneespace vanity, whirlpool tub, and walk-in closet.

plan⊕ HPT7600068

Style: Italianate
First Floor: 1,671 sq. ft.
Second Floor: 846 sq. ft.
Total: 2,517 sq. ft.
Bonus Space: 140 sq. ft.
Bedrooms: 3
Bathrooms: 2
Width: 44' - 0"
Depth: 55' - 0"
Foundation: Basement

SEARCH ONLINE @ EPLANS.COM

BASEMENT

FIRST FLOOR

SECOND FLOOR

ORDER BLUEPRINTS 24 HOURS, 7 DAYS A WEEK, AT 1-800-521-6797

Style: Italianate

First Floor: 1,855 sq. ft.

Second Floor: 901 sq. ft.

Total: 2,756 sq. ft.

Bonus Space: 1,010 sq. ft.

Bedrooms: 3½

Bathrooms: 3½

Width: 66' - 0"

Depth: 50' - 0"

Foundation: Basement

SEARCH ONLINE @ EPLANS.COM

Villa enchantment is romantically enhanced by the facade of this Italianate design. Enter through double doors to the two-story foyer—notice the study with built-in cabinetry to the right and the formal dining room to the left. Straight ahead, an octagonal great room with a multifaceted vaulted ceiling illuminates the entire plan. Two spacious walk-in closets and a whirlpool tub await to pamper the homeowner in the master suite. A U-shaped staircase winds upstairs to a loft, which overlooks the great room and the foyer. Two additional family bedrooms each feature private baths. A computer center and a morning kitchen are located at the end of the hallway, before opening to the outer deck.

SECOND FLOOR

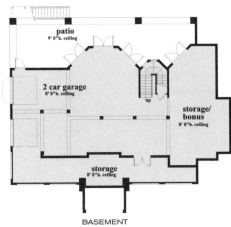

BASEMENT

FIRST FLOOR

master deck

SECOND FLOOR

plan# HPT7600070

Style: Italianate
First Floor: 2,039 sq. ft.
Second Floor: 1,426 sq. ft.
Total: 3,465 sq. ft.
Bedrooms: 3
Bathrooms: 4
Width: 56' - 0"
Depth: 54' - 0"
Foundation: Basement

SEARCH ONLINE @ EPLANS.COM

A stunning transom creates a picture-perfect entry and a glorious complement to the arch-top windows with this exquisite villa. Double stairs embraced by a classic balustrade lead to a midlevel landing, easing the transition from ground level to the front door. The foyer opens to a central gallery, which enjoys extensive views through the interior.

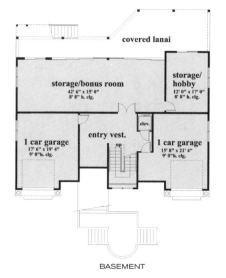

BASEMENT

FIRST FLOOR

SECOND FLOOR

plan# HPT7600071

Style: Italianate
First Floor: 1,542 sq. ft.
Second Floor: 971 sq. ft.
Total: 2,513 sq. ft.
Bedrooms: 3
Bathrooms: 3
Width: 46' - 0"
Depth: 51' - 0"
Foundation: Basement

SEARCH ONLINE @ EPLANS.COM

Stately and elegant, this home displays fine Tuscan columns, fanlight windows, hipped gables, and a detailed balustrade that splash its facade with a subtle European flavor. Inside, a dramatic winding staircase provides a focal point to the grand entry. The foyer opens to the true heart of this home, the two-story great room. With imaginative angles and French doors, the great room holds a magnificent fireplace nestled with built-in cabinetry. A secluded study is perfectly suited for quiet moments of reflection and intimate entertaining. The formal dining room boasts a fabulous view of the outdoors as well as access to the expansive covered porch via French doors.

BASEMENT

FIRST FLOOR

Multiple windows bring natural light to this beautiful home, which offers a floor plan filled with special amenities. Arches provide a grand entry to the beam-ceilinged great room, where built-ins flank the fireplace and three sets of French doors open to a veranda. Step ceilings grace the master suite and the dining room. The master suite provides two walk-in closets and a resplendent bath; dazzling windows in the dining room allow enjoyment of the outdoors. Two second-floor bedrooms, one with a sundeck, feature walk-in closets and private baths.

plan # HPT7600072

Style: Italianate
First Floor: 2,096 sq. ft.
Second Floor: 892 sq. ft.
Total: 2,988 sq. ft.
Bedrooms: 3
Bathrooms: 3½
Width: 56' - 0"
Depth: 54' - 0"
Foundation: Basement

SEARCH ONLINE @ EPLANS.COM

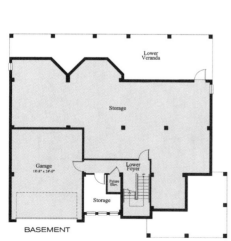

BASEMENT

FIRST FLOOR

SECOND FLOOR

© The Sater Design Collection, Inc.

plan # HPT7600073

Style: Spanish
Square Footage: 3,351
Bedrooms: 3
Bathrooms: 2½ + ½
Width: 84' - 0"
Depth: 92' - 2"
Foundation: Slab

SEARCH ONLINE @ EPLANS.COM

A Spanish beauty, this stucco estate is striking with its red-roof tiles and grand entry. Inside, an expansive living room/dining room combination features a rustic exposed-beam ceiling, fireplace, and built-in shelving. An angled country kitchen allows plenty of workspace and an open design. The bayed nook would be a bright breakfast area or reading spot. The leisure room will be a family favorite with a built-in entertainment center and access to the rear veranda and outdoor grill. Secluded for ultimate privacy, the master suite will elate; a bay window, walk-in closets, and a pampering spa bath are thoughtful touches.

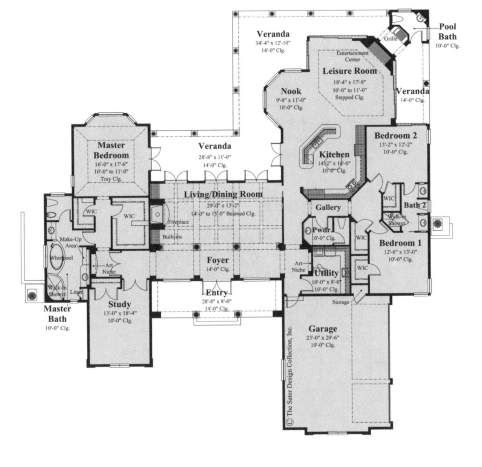

© The Sater Design Collection, Inc.

European stylings and beautiful windows present a lovely facade. Inside, a grand entry reveals a modern floor plan that fits today's family and your busy lifestyle. Elegant ceiling treatments throughout bring splendor to every room in the home. The great room soars with a vaulted beamed ceiling for vintage appeal. A lateral fireplace allows for sweeping rear views; French doors provide access to the lanai. The open dining room leads to a spacious country kitchen, adorned with a charming bayed nook. The first-floor master suite is a dream come true; a bayed window and a whirlpool tub set in a turret are exquisite touches. French doors lead to a private lanai. Upstairs, two generous bedrooms share a full bath and deck access. A bonus room with a full bath can be finished as your needs change.

plan# HPT7600074

Style: Italianate
First Floor: 2,250 sq. ft.
Second Floor: 663 sq. ft.
Total: 2,913 sq. ft.
Bonus Space: 351 sq. ft.
Bedrooms: 3
Bathrooms: 3½
Width: 72' - 0"
Depth: 68' - 3"
Foundation: Slab

SEARCH ONLINE @ EPLANS.COM

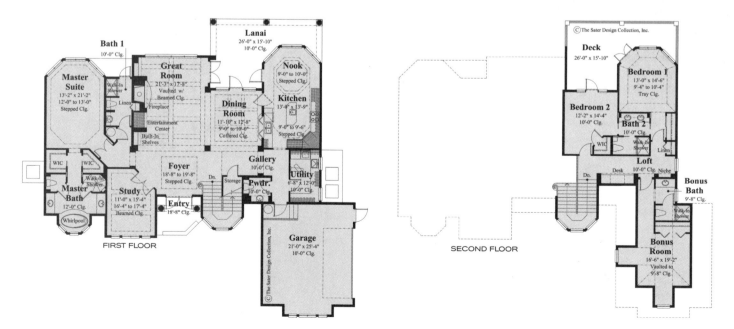

ORDER BLUEPRINTS 24 HOURS, 7 DAYS A WEEK, AT 1-800-521-6797

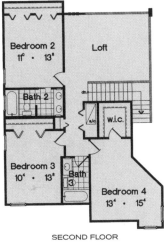

plan # HPT7600075

Style: Mediterranean
First Floor: 1,844 sq. ft.
Second Floor: 1,017 sq. ft.
Total: 2,861 sq. ft.
Bedrooms: 4
Bathrooms: 3½
Width: 45' - 0"
Depth: 67' - 8"
Foundation: Slab

SEARCH ONLINE @ EPLANS.COM

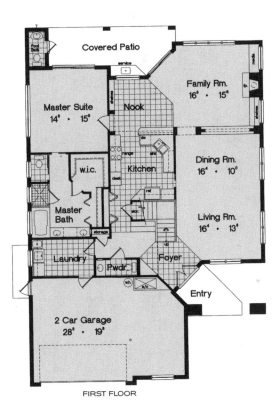

The excitement begins upon entering the foyer of this home where an impressive staircase is its focal point. Just off the nook is a sliding glass door to the covered patio where a wet bar can be found as well as a pool bath. The gourmet kitchen is conveniently located at the heart of the home for easy access. The master suite is generously sized and features a wonderful wall of high transom glass, as well as sliding glass doors to the patio—note the lavish private bath with a large walk-in closet and dual vanities. A spacious loft works well as a game room, study, or library—or it can be a fifth bedroom.

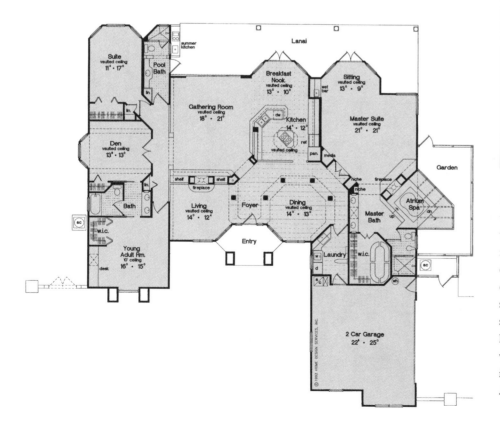

plan # HPT7600076

Style: Mediterranean
Square Footage: 3,280
Bedrooms: 3
Bathrooms: 3
Width: 72' - 4"
Depth: 82' - 0"
Foundation: Slab

SEARCH ONLINE @ EPLANS.COM

Mediterranean splendor abounds as you enter under the tiered portico. The foyer opens to the living room on the left and the dining room on the right where attention to details—columns and soffits—create elegance and excitement. The living and gathering rooms share a see-through fireplace, and beyond the sliding glass doors, the lanai offers a summer kitchen. The magnificent master suite offers a wet bar in the bayed sittiing area. A solarium is, however, the focal point here with an African spa and through fireplace.

plan# HPT7600077

Style: Mediterranean
Square Footage: 2,747
Bedrooms: 4
Bathrooms: 4½
Width: 74' - 4"
Depth: 83' - 2"
Foundation: Basement

SEARCH ONLINE @ EPLANS.COM

The towering entry of this stucco beauty makes for a gracious entrance to the floor plan inside. Double doors open off the covered front porch to a dining room and a living room defined by columns. A fireplace warms the living room. To the back are the casual areas: a family room, breakfast nook and gourmet kitchen. A bedroom with a full bath and the utility area sit directly behind the two-car garage. The master suite features a study and private bath. The lower level can be developed into a recreation room or additional bedroom suites.

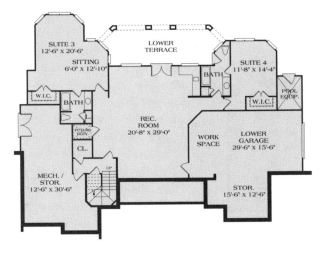

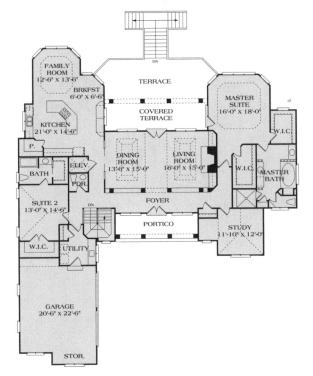

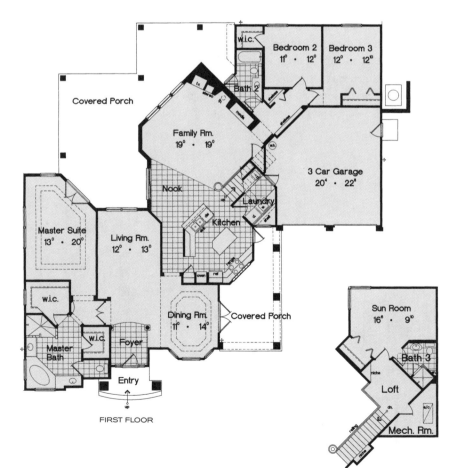

FIRST FLOOR

Sun Room
16⁰ · 9⁰

Bath 3

Loft

Mech. Rm.

SECOND FLOOR

plan# HPT7600008

Style: Mediterranean
First Floor: 2,365 sq. ft.
Second Floor: 364 sq. ft.
Total: 2,729 sq. ft.
Bedrooms: 3
Bathrooms: 3
Width: 69' - 0"
Depth: 70' - 0"
Foundation: Slab

SEARCH ONLINE @ EPLANS.COM

The columned foyer of this home welcomes you into a series of spaces that reach out in all directions. The living room has a spectacular view of the huge covered patio area that's perfect for summer entertaining. The dining room features a tray ceiling and French doors that lead to a covered porch. A secluded master suite affords great views through French doors and also has a tray ceiling. The family wing combines an island kitchen, nook, and family gathering space, with the built-in media/fireplace wall the center of attention. Two secondary bedrooms share a bath. A staircase overlooking the family room takes you up to the sunroom complete with a full bath.

ORDER BLUEPRINTS 24 HOURS, 7 DAYS A WEEK, AT 1-800-521-6797

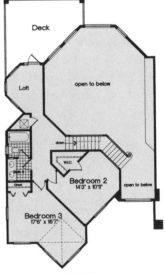

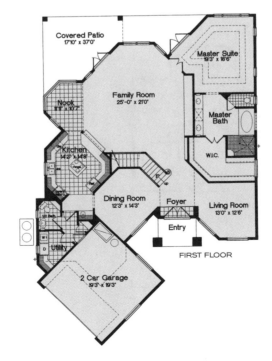

plan# HPT7600078

Style: Mediterranean
First Floor: 2,051 sq. ft.
Second Floor: 749 sq. ft.
Total: 2,800 sq. ft.
Bedrooms: 3
Bathrooms: 2½
Width: 50' - 0"
Depth: 74' - 0"
Foundation: Slab

SEARCH ONLINE @ EPLANS.COM

Only 50 feet wide, this fabulous design will fit anywhere! From the moment you enter the home from the foyer, this floor plan explodes in every direction with huge living spaces. Flanking the foyer are the living and dining rooms. Ahead, the visual impact of the staircase is breathtaking. Two-story ceilings adorn the huge family room with double-stacked glass walls. Sunlight floods the breakfast nook, and the kitchen is a gourmet's dream, complete with a cooking island and loads of overhead cabinets. Tray ceilings grace the master suite, which also offers a well-designed private bath. Here, a large soaking tub, doorless shower, private toilet chamber, and huge walk-in closet are sure to please. Upstairs, two oversized bedrooms and a loft space—perfect for the home computer—share a full bath.

Stone and stucco bring a chateau welcome to this Mediterranean-style home. A sensational sunroom lights up the rear of the plan and flows to the bayed breakfast nook. The living area opens to the formal dining room. A master suite with rear-deck access leads to a family or guest bedroom with a private bath. Upstairs, two secondary bedrooms and a full bath enjoy easy kitchen access down a side stairway.

plan # HPT7600079

Style: Mediterranean
First Floor: 2,502 sq. ft.
Second Floor: 677 sq. ft.
Total: 3,179 sq. ft.
Bonus Space: 171 sq. ft.
Bedrooms: 4
Bathrooms: 3½
Width: 71' - 2"
Depth: 56' - 10"
Foundation: Walkout Basement

SEARCH ONLINE @ EPLANS.COM

FIRST FLOOR

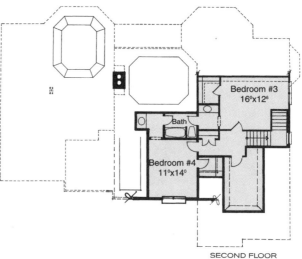

SECOND FLOOR

ORDER BLUEPRINTS 24 HOURS, 7 DAYS A WEEK, AT 1-800-521-6797

plan# HPT7600080

Style: French Country
First Floor: 1,840 sq. ft.
Second Floor: 840 sq. ft.
Total: 2,680 sq. ft.
Bonus Space: 295 sq. ft.
Bedrooms: 3
Bathrooms: 2½
Width: 66' - 0"
Depth: 65' - 10"
Foundation: Crawlspace

SEARCH ONLINE @ EPLANS.COM

Multipane windows, shutters, and shingle accents adorn the stucco facade of this wonderful French Country home. Inside, the foyer introduces the hearth-warmed great room that features French-door access to the rear deck. The dining room, defined from the foyer and great room by columns, enjoys front-yard views. The master bedroom includes two walk-in closets, rear-deck access, and a dual-vanity bath. The informal living areas have an open plan. The box-bayed breakfast nook joins the cooktop-island kitchen and hearth-warmed family room. The second floor holds two bedrooms with walk-in closets, a study, and an unfinished bedroom for future expansion.

SECOND FLOOR

FIRST FLOOR

A beautiful one-story turret is accompanied by arched windows and a stucco facade. A terrific casual combination of kitchen, breakfast area, and a vaulted keeping room provide space for family gatherings. Both the keeping room and great room sport cheery fireplaces. The master suite is secluded on the first floor. This relaxing retreat offers a sitting room, His and Hers walk-in closets, dual vanities, and compartmented toilet. Two family bedrooms share a full bath on the second floor. An optional bonus room can be used as a game room or home office.

plan # HPT7600081

Style: Mediterranean
First Floor: 1,972 sq. ft.
Second Floor: 579 sq. ft.
Total: 2,551 sq. ft.
Bonus Space: 256 sq. ft.
Bedrooms: 3
Bathrooms: 2½
Width: 57' - 4"
Depth: 51' - 2"
Foundation: Crawlspace,
Basement, Slab

SEARCH ONLINE @ EPLANS.COM

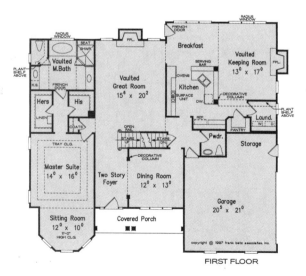

FIRST FLOOR

SECOND FLOOR

ORDER BLUEPRINTS 24 HOURS, 7 DAYS A WEEK, AT 1-800-521-6797

plan# HPT7600082

Style: French Country
Square Footage: 3,049
Bonus Space: 868 sq. ft.
Bedrooms: 3
Bathrooms: 2½
Width: 72' - 6"
Depth: 78' - 10"
Foundation: Basement, Crawlspace

SEARCH ONLINE @ EPLANS.COM

This charming home, with its brick exterior and Old World accents, seems to have been plucked from the English countryside. The arched entry opens to the two-story foyer with a balcony overlook. The formal dining room sits on the left, and the living room is on the right. Beyond the elegant staircase, the family room offers a magnificent view of the backyard. Off to the left is the sunny breakfast alcove and the adjoining kitchen. A split-bedroom design places the master suite on the left and two family bedrooms on the right. An optional second floor allows for two more bedrooms, two additional baths, and a recreation room.

Inviting Villas

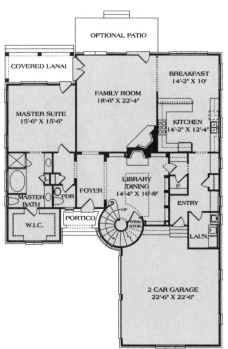

FIRST FLOOR

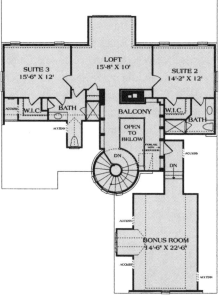

SECOND FLOOR

plan # HPT7600083

Style: French
First Floor: 1,980 sq. ft.
Second Floor: 1,186 sq. ft.
Total: 3,166 sq. ft.
Bonus Space: 433 sq. ft.
Bedrooms: 3
Bathrooms: 3½
Width: 50' - 8"
Depth: 69' - 0"
Foundation: Crawlspace

SEARCH ONLINE @ EPLANS.COM

A central turret highlights this lovely French Country home. A corner fireplace warms the family room, where French doors open to a covered lanai and an additional door opens to an optional patio. Another fireplace enhances the library/dining room, which boasts nearby wine storage. Luxury reigns in the first-floor master suite, with its private bath and spacious walk-in closet; two additional bedrooms, each with private baths, share a loft on the second floor.

plan # HPT7600084

Style: French Country
First Floor: 1,805 sq. ft.
Second Floor: 952 sq. ft.
Total: 2,757 sq. ft.
Bonus Space: 475 sq. ft.
Bedrooms: 4
Bathrooms: 3½
Width: 48' - 10"
Depth: 64' - 10"
Foundation: Crawlspace, Basement

SEARCH ONLINE @ EPLANS.COM

The European allure of this stunning two-story home will be the delight of the neighborhood. With the living room to the right, the foyer leads to the family room with a magnificent view of the outdoors. The island kitchen is thoughtfully situated between the sunny breakfast area and the formal dining room, which opens to the side terrace. The master suite finds privacy on the first floor; the three family bedrooms share two full baths on the second floor.

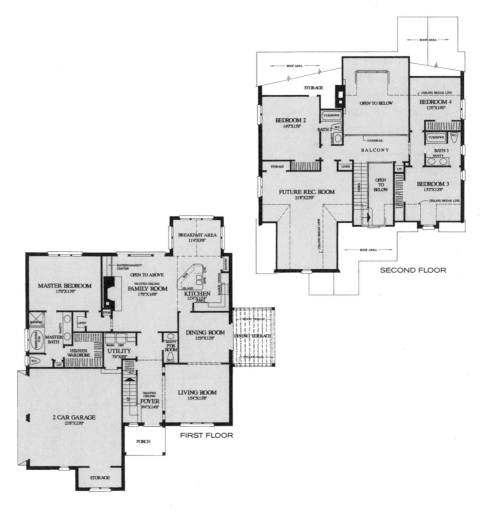

French influence is highly evident on this fine three-bedroom home. From the hipped rooflines to the delicate detailing on the dormers and around the door, this house is full of class. Inside, the foyer introduces the formal living room, which opens to the formal dining room just off the kitchen. The beam-ceilinged family room offers a fireplace, built-ins, and a wonderful view of the backyard. Two family bedrooms, sharing a bath, and a lavish master suite with a private bath complete this floor. Upstairs is all bonus space, perfect for future expansion.

plan # HPT7600085

Style: French
Square Footage: 2,717
Bonus Space: 1,133 sq. ft.
Bedrooms: 3
Bathrooms: 2½
Width: 68' - 6"
Depth: 79' - 10"
Foundation: Crawlspace, Basement

SEARCH ONLINE @ EPLANS.COM

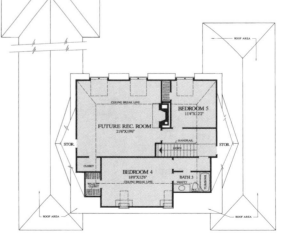

ORDER BLUEPRINTS 24 HOURS, 7 DAYS A WEEK, AT 1-800-521-6797

plan # HPT7600086

Style: French
First Floor: 2,216 sq. ft.
Second Floor: 1,192 sq. ft.
Total: 3,408 sq. ft.
Bonus Space: 458 sq. ft.
Bedrooms: 4
Bathrooms: 3½
Width: 67' - 10"
Depth: 56' - 10"
Foundation: Crawlspace

SEARCH ONLINE @ EPLANS.COM

This elegant, tasteful chateau charms and delights, with an Old World flavor and a balcony that will inspire Shakespearean soliloquies. The foyer is flanked by the formal living room and dining room. The expansive kitchen is conveniently situated to serve both dining and breakfast areas with ease. The comforting family room offers a marvelous view and an enchanting fireplace. The master suite finds privacy on the first floor near a secondary stairway on the left. An additional bedroom suite is found on the second floor, along with two more bedrooms, a full bath, and space for a future rec room.

SECOND FLOOR

FIRST FLOOR

Inviting Villas

Storybook rooflines and a decorative Italian balcony bring Old World style to this New World design. Arched windows surround the home and fill it with natural light. Enter past the portico—front or rear—to a beautiful floor plan. The U-shaped kitchen features an island workspace and easy access to both the columned dining room and the informal breakfast nook, as well as convenient access to the utility room and garage. The master suite includes a spacious walk-in closet and His and Hers vanities. Upstairs, two family suites, each with its own bath and walk-in closet, share a loft.

plan # HPT7600087

Style: French
First Floor: 2,055 sq. ft.
Second Floor: 935 sq. ft.
Total: 2,990 sq. ft.
Bedrooms: 4
Bathrooms: 4
Width: 65' - 5"
Depth: 55' - 10"
Foundation: Crawlspace

SEARCH ONLINE @ EPLANS.COM

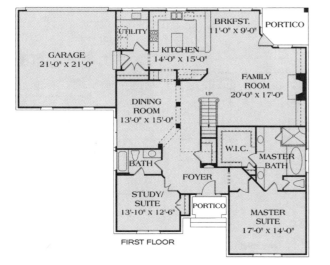

FIRST FLOOR

SECOND FLOOR

ORDER BLUEPRINTS 24 HOURS, 7 DAYS A WEEK, AT 1-800-521-6797

plan # HPT7600088

Style: French
First Floor: 2,250 sq. ft.
Second Floor: 1,180 sq. ft.
Total: 3,430 sq. ft.
Bonus Space: 438 sq. ft.
Bedrooms: 5
Bathrooms: 3½
Width: 76' - 3"
Depth: 95' - 7"
Foundation: Slab

SEARCH ONLINE @ EPLANS.COM

This two-story French Country classic is perfect for the large family that likes a formal setting. As you enter this beauty, you face the grand stairway. The formal living room, den, and master suite sit to the right. To the left is the formal dining room and the family areas. The hallway to the master suite passes a powder room that offers access to the patio area. The master bath offers dual vanities, a large walk-in closet, a soaking tub, and a private toilet chamber. The kitchen, overlooking the breakfast nook and family room, is a dream with its cooktop island and large pantry. The second floor of this home provides four bedrooms and two full baths.

FIRST FLOOR

SECOND FLOOR

European hospitality comes to mind with this home's high hipped roof, arched dormers, and welcoming front porch. This clever and original two-story plan begins with the foyer opening to the staircase. At the end of the foyer, a spacious great room provides built-ins, a warming fireplace, and double doors leading to the deck. The kitchen has excellent accommodations for preparation of meals, and the keeping room (with access to the deck) will make family gatherings comfortable. Note the storage space, powder room, and pantry near the two-car garage. Inside the master suite, an enormous walk-in closet divides the bath, with its own shower, garden tub, and double-bowl vanity.

plan# HPT7600089

Style: French
First Floor: 2,060 sq. ft.
Second Floor: 926 sq. ft.
Total: 2,986 sq. ft.
Bedrooms: 4
Bathrooms: 3½
Width: 86' - 0"
Depth: 65' - 5"
Foundation: Crawlspace

SEARCH ONLINE @ EPLANS.COM

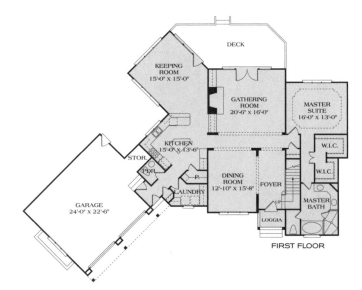

FIRST FLOOR

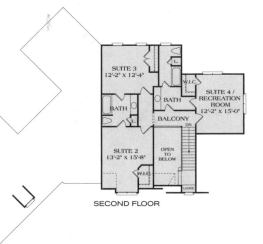

SECOND FLOOR

plan # HPT7600090

Style: French
First Floor: 2,391 sq. ft.
Second Floor: 1,071 sq. ft.
Total: 3,462 sq. ft.
Bedrooms: 3
Bathrooms: 3½
Width: 113' - 7"
Depth: 57' - 5"
Foundation: Crawlspace

SEARCH ONLINE @ EPLANS.COM

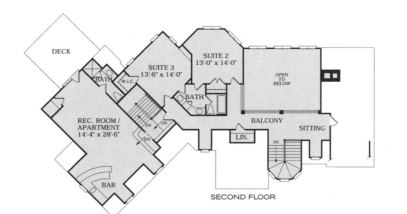

SECOND FLOOR

If you've ever dreamed of living in a castle, this could be the home for you. The interior is also fit for royalty, from the formal dining room to the multipurpose grand room to the comfortable sitting area off the kitchen. The master suite has its own fireplace, two walk-in closets, and a compartmented bath with dual vanities and a garden tub. Two stairways lead to the second floor. One, housed in the turret, leads to a sitting area and a balcony overlooking the grand room. The balcony leads to two more bedrooms and a recreation room (or apartment) with a deck.

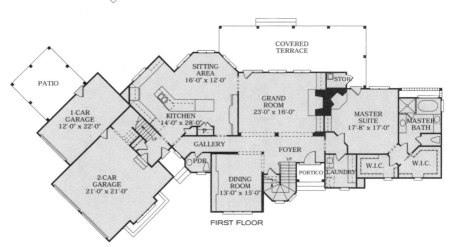

FIRST FLOOR

Open To Below

Open To Below

Bedroom No. 2
12³ x 14⁹

Bedroom No. 3
10⁹ x 14⁰

SECOND FLOOR

plan# HPT7600005

Style: Mediterranean
First Floor: 2,058 sq. ft.
Second Floor: 712 sq. ft.
Total: 2,770 sq. ft.
Bedrooms: 3
Bathrooms: 2½
Width: 57' - 3"
Depth: 81' - 3"
Foundation: Crawlspace

SEARCH ONLINE @ EPLANS.COM

Master Bedroom
15³ x 19³

Terrace

Great Room
25⁰ x 20³

Kitchen
17⁰ x 12⁰

Dining Room
12⁰ x 12⁰

Foyer

FIRST FLOOR

Two Car Garage
22⁰ x 28³

If you've always dreamed of owning a villa, we invite you to experience this European lifestyle—on a perfectly manageable scale. This home offers the best of traditional formality and casual elegance. The foyer leads to the great room, with a bold but stylish fireplace and three French doors to the rear terrace—sure to be left open during fair weather. The large kitchen opens gracefully to a private dining room that has access to a covered outdoor patio. The master suite combines great views and a sumptuous bath to complete this winning design. Upstairs, a balcony hall overlooking the great room leads to two family bedrooms that share a full hall bath.

plan# HPT7600091

Style: Mediterranean
First Floor: 1,805 sq. ft.
Second Floor: 765 sq. ft.
Total: 2,570 sq. ft.
Bonus Space: 140 sq. ft.
Bedrooms: 3
Bathrooms: 2½
Width: 60' - 6"
Depth: 56' - 6"
Foundation: Walkout Basement

SEARCH ONLINE @ EPLANS.COM

Stone and stucco, with the delicate addition of a latticed front porch, present this home with a gracious welcome. Open living spaces invite casual times in the expansive great room with a full measure of windows and a fireplace rising the full two stories. An adjoining breakfast room with patio doors provides a casual place for meals with easy access from the kitchen. From the gourmet kitchen, the formal dining room is served through a rear passage. The secluded master bedroom enjoys a spacious bath highlighted with a spa tub and a walk-in closet. Upstairs, the balcony hall that overlooks the great room leads to a loft and two secondary bedrooms that share a bath.

Baronial in attitude, the Chateau style reflects the Renaissance elegance of its namesake castles in France. Here, the basic formality of the Chateau style has been purposely mellowed for modern-day living: the roof line is simplified, and massive masonry construction is replaced by a stucco finish. However, none of the drama has been lost in the translation. The two-story foyer is made for grand entrances, with a marble floor and a sweeping staircase. The foyer opens to the formal dining room and leads to the great room with its fireplace, vaulted ceiling and wet bar. Also located on the first floor is the master suite, which has twin walk-in closets. A quaint keeping room with a fireplace adjoins the kitchen and breakfast areas. Upstairs you will find three generous bedrooms and two baths, one private, plus a bonus room.

plan # HPT7600092

Style: French
First Floor: 2,357 sq. ft.
Second Floor: 1,021 sq. ft.
Total: 3,378 sq. ft.
Bonus Space: 168 sq. ft.
Bedrooms: 4
Bathrooms: 3½
Width: 70' - 0"
Depth: 62' - 6"
Foundation: Walkout Basement

SEARCH ONLINE @ EPLANS.COM

FIRST FLOOR

SECOND FLOOR

ORDER BLUEPRINTS 24 HOURS, 7 DAYS A WEEK, AT 1-800-521-6797

plan# HPT7600093

Style: French
First Floor: 1,980 sq. ft.
Second Floor: 1,317 sq. ft.
Total: 3,297 sq. ft.
Bonus Space: 255 sq. ft.
Bedrooms: 4
Bathrooms: 3½
Width: 58' - 9"
Depth: 66' - 9"
Foundation: Walkout Basement

SEARCH ONLINE @ EPLANS.COM

Centuries ago, the center column played a vital role in the support of a double-arched window such as the one that graces this home's exterior. Today's amenities combined with the well-seasoned architecture of Europe offer the best of both worlds. The contemporary floor plan begins with a soaring foyer that opens onto the formal living and dining rooms. Casual living is enjoyed at the rear of the plan in the L-shaped kitchen, the family room, and the light-filled breakfast/sunroom. A guest bedroom is tucked behind the family room for privacy. Upstairs, an exquisite master suite features a lavish bath and a huge walk-in closet. Two family bedrooms, a full bath, and unfinished bonus space complete the second floor.

FIRST FLOOR

SECOND FLOOR

Quaint, yet majestic, this European-style stucco home enjoys the enchantment of arched windows to underscore its charm. The two-story foyer leads through French doors to the study with its own hearth and coffered ceiling. Coupled with this cozy sanctuary is the master suite with a tray ceiling and large accommodating bath. The large sunken great room is highlighted by a fireplace, built-in bookcases, lots of glass, and easy access to a back stair and large gourmet kitchen. Three secondary bedrooms reside upstairs. One upstairs bedroom gives guests a private bath and walk-in closet.

plan # HPT7600094

Style: French
First Floor: 2,208 sq. ft.
Second Floor: 1,250 sq. ft.
Total: 3,458 sq. ft.
Bedrooms: 4
Bathrooms: 3½
Width: 60' - 6"
Depth: 60' - 0"
Foundation: Walkout Basement

SEARCH ONLINE @ EPLANS.COM

QUOTE ONE®
Cost to build? See page 187
to order complete cost estimate
to build this house in your area!

FIRST FLOOR

SECOND FLOOR

plan # HPT7600095

Style: Mediterranean
First Floor: 1,475 sq. ft.
Second Floor: 1,460 sq. ft.
Total: 2,935 sq. ft.
Bedrooms: 4
Bathrooms: 3½
Width: 57' - 6"
Depth: 46' - 6"
Foundation: Walkout Basement

SEARCH ONLINE @ EPLANS.COM

French-entry doors open to a formal dining room on the left with excellent frontal views, and a formal living room on the right that leads to a quiet corner media room. The bayed great room offers access to the rear deck in order to enjoy the full benefits of sun and outdoor activities. A large island kitchen with a bayed breakfast nook completes the first floor of this plan. Upstairs, Bedrooms 2 and 3 share a full bath, and Bedroom 4 includes it own bath. The master bedroom features a bayed sitting area and an exquisite master bath with a wonderful vanity area, massive walk-in closet, and unique step-up tub.

SECOND FLOOR

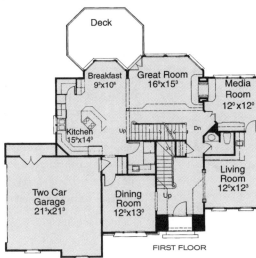

FIRST FLOOR

HOLZHAUER INC.

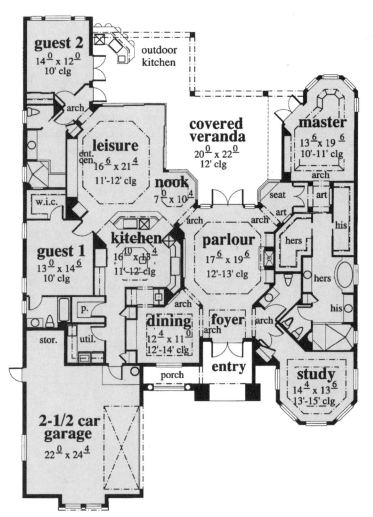

plan# HPT7600096

Style: Italianate
Square Footage: 3,230
Bedrooms: 3
Bathrooms: 3½
Width: 65' - 0"
Depth: 94' - 10"
Foundation: Slab

SEARCH ONLINE @ EPLANS.COM

A majestic entry introduces this charming Mediterranean manor. The central parlor, with arches at each entry, features French doors that open to the rear veranda. Nearby, the kitchen accesses the dining room through a handy butler's pantry. The master suite, to the right of the plan, features a bayed sitting area plus His and Hers walk-in closets and vanities. To the left of the plan, two additional suites include special amenities— one opens to the veranda and outdoor kitchen, and the other boasts a private bath.

Grand Estates

This manor would be a stunning centerpiece to any grand estate. See more on page 180.

This inviting entrance opens to a romantic foyer with double staircases. The gathering room and dining room are directly behind the staircases, and off to each side is a master suite. Each features a private bath and walk-in closet. The first floor also offers a home theater and an exercise room. Upstairs, off the balcony and loft, are two private suites with an office extending from each one. Notice that the entrance is flanked by two two-car garages.

plan# HPT7600098

Style: French
First Floor: 3,662 sq. ft.
Second Floor: 2,456 sq. ft.
Total: 6,118 sq. ft.
Bedrooms: 4
Bathrooms: 4½
Width: 85' - 10"
Depth: 88' - 11"
Foundation: Crawlspace

SEARCH ONLINE @ EPLANS.COM

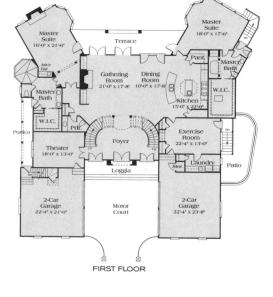

FIRST FLOOR

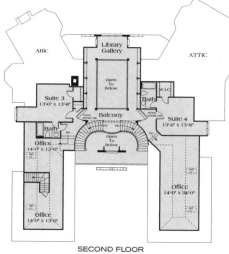

SECOND FLOOR

Grand Estates

plan# HPT7600099

Style: French
First Floor: 3,420 sq. ft.
Second Floor: 2,076 sq. ft.
Total: 5,496 sq. ft.
Bonus Space: 721 sq. ft.
Bedrooms: 4
Bathrooms: 5½ + ½
Width: 85' - 6"
Depth: 102' - 6"
Foundation: Crawlspace

SEARCH ONLINE @ EPLANS.COM

Classic French elements along with style and balance give this home great curb appeal. The foyer leads to the gallery and on to the grand room, complete with its bank of windows, a fireplace, and built-ins. Two more fireplaces can be found in the family room and the study, off the foyer. A secondary staircase leads from the kitchen/breakfast area to the recreational room on the second level. A pool room and office are tucked over the garage, and three bedroom suites and four full baths complete this floor. The master suite is located on the first level, allowing for privacy.

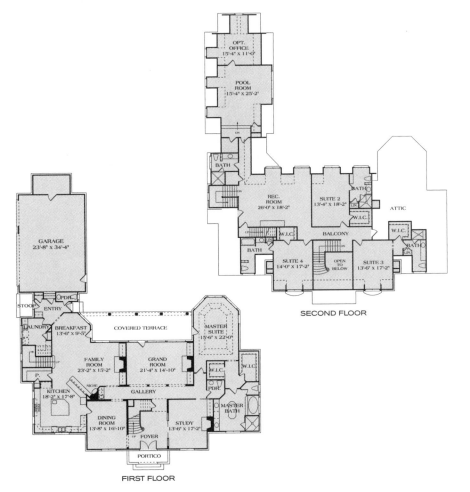

SECOND FLOOR

FIRST FLOOR

Grand Estates

Three arches and three gables highlight the entrance facade of this beautiful stucco four-bedroom home. Inside, a formal dining room and a study/living room flank a two-story foyer. Directly ahead is a spacious gathering room, complete with a fireplace and direct access to the rear deck/terrace. Unique angles enhance the island kitchen, which features a walk-in pantry, a planning desk, and a snack bar into the adjacent morning room. Located on the first floor for privacy, the master suite is sure to please with its many amenities, which include a walk-in closet, sumptuous master bath, and access to the rear deck/terrace. Upstairs, there are three suites—each with a walk-in closet—and a studio that would be great for a computer room, study room, or kids' media room.

plan# HPT7600100

Style: French
First Floor: 2,373 sq. ft.
Second Floor: 1,402 sq. ft.
Total: 3,775 sq. ft.
Bedrooms: 4
Bathrooms: 3½
Width: 82' - 0"
Depth: 68' - 0"
Foundation: Crawlspace

SEARCH ONLINE @ EPLANS.COM

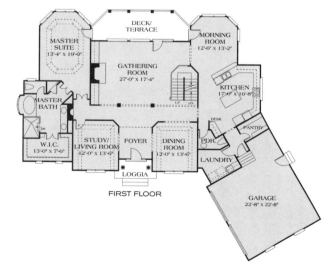

FIRST FLOOR

SECOND FLOOR

ORDER BLUEPRINTS 24 HOURS, 7 DAYS A WEEK, AT 1-800-521-6797

plan # HPT7600101

Style: Mediterranean
First Floor: 2,943 sq. ft.
Second Floor: 1,510 sq. ft.
Total: 4,453 sq. ft.
Bedrooms: 4
Bathrooms: 3½
Width: 104' - 2"
Depth: 78' - 1"
Foundation: Basement

SEARCH ONLINE @ EPLANS.COM

This palatial European design offers all the beauty and excitement of Mediterranean style. Stately columns frame the portico, which offers entry into the raised foyer. To the right, the master wing offers a suite filled with pampering delights. The first-floor location of the suite ensures privacy and includes a bright sitting bay, lavish bath, double walk-in closet, and shares a see-through fireplace with the living room. The gourmet kitchen provides an island and serves the dining room and morning nook with ease. The gathering room is a casual retreat warmed by a second fireplace, accessing the terrace and screened porch. The captain's quarters and three other suites reside upstairs.

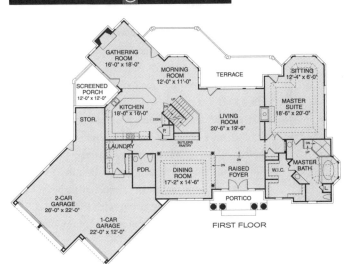

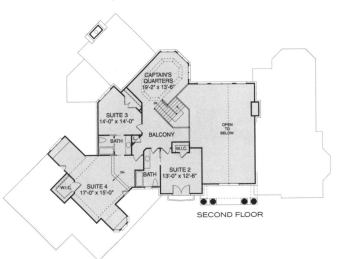

Grand Estates

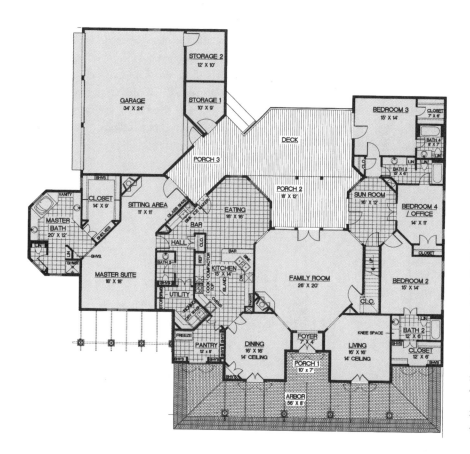

plan # HPT7600102

Style: French
Square Footage: 3,960
Bedrooms: 4
Bathrooms: 4½
Width: 96' - 0"
Depth: 90' - 0"
Foundation: Crawlspace, Basement, Slab

SEARCH ONLINE @ EPLANS.COM

A hipped roofline, with varying elevations, accents this stunning Mediterranean design and lends superb curb appeal. Double doors in the uniquely shaped family room open to the rear porch and deck. The large family room, complete with a corner fireplace, is accessible from all points of the house—kitchen area, deck, dining room, living room, and the hallway leading to the sleeping quarters on the right side of the plan—creating a perfect hub of activity. The master suite features a private bath, a large walk-in closet, and a sitting room with a fireplace. The three-car garage holds a convenient storage area.

ORDER BLUEPRINTS 24 HOURS, 7 DAYS A WEEK, AT 1-800-521-6797

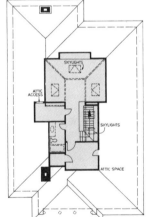

BONUS SPACE

two-car
garage
20' x 20'6

A contemporary classic with Mediterranean flair, this beautiful home will be the envy of any community. Follow the formal foyer to the right, where an elegant living room is graced with columns, a gas fireplace, and triplet French doors topped by sunbursts, leading out to the terrace. A private den includes storage space, making it a great home office. In the casual family room, a gas fireplace warms and saves energy. A spiral staircase leads to the balcony overlook above and the family quarters. Three bedroom suites enjoy private baths; the master suite is full of natural light and relishes an indulgent bath. A second staircase leads back down to the foyer.

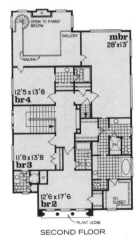

SECOND FLOOR

FIRST FLOOR

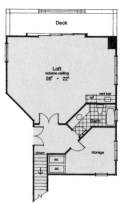

Deck

Loft
volume ceiling
28' • 22'

ref

wet bar

Bath

down

storage

ac

ac

SECOND FLOOR

FIRST FLOOR

---

plan # HPT7600104

Style: Mediterranean
First Floor: 3,395 sq. ft.
Second Floor: 757 sq. ft.
Total: 4,152 sq. ft.
Bedrooms: 3
Bathrooms: 3½
Width: 71' - 0"
Depth: 100' - 8"
Foundation: Slab

SEARCH ONLINE @ EPLANS.COM

Old World Mediterranean flavor spills over and combines with classic contemporary lines through the courtyard and at the double-door entry to this three-bedroom home. The formal living room is defined by columns and a glass wall that looks out over the rear patio. The formal dining room offers access to the front courtyard with French doors. A den/library also has French doors to the courtyard and accesses the pool bath for the occasional guest. Double doors bring you into the world of the master suite and sumptuous luxury. A lavish bath features a soaking tub, glass-enclosed shower and His and Hers walk-in closets. Two large family bedrooms, both with bay windows, share a full bath. A spectacular loft awaits upstairs to accommodate a home theater, game room or bedroom.

© The Sater Design Collection, Inc.

plan # HPT7600105

Style: Mediterranean
First Floor: 2,850 sq. ft.
Second Floor: 1,155 sq. ft.
Total: 4,005 sq. ft.
Bonus Space: 371 sq. ft.
Bedrooms: 4
Bathrooms: 4½
Width: 71' - 6"
Depth: 83' - 0"
Foundation: Slab

SEARCH ONLINE @ EPLANS.COM

Stone, stucco, and soaring rooflines combine to give this elegant Mediterranean design a stunning exterior. The interior is packed with luxurious amenities, from the wall of glass in the living room to the whirlpool tub in the master bath. A dining room and study serve as formal areas, while a leisure room with a fireplace offers a relaxing retreat. The first-floor master suite boasts a private bayed sitting area. Upstairs, all three bedrooms include private baths; Bedroom 2 and the guest suite also provide walk-in closets.

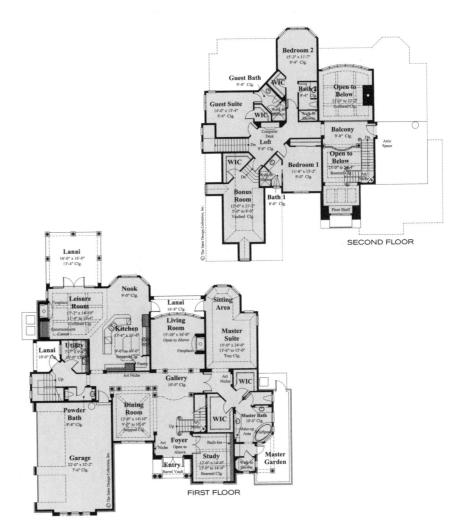

The striking facade of this magnificent estate is just the beginning of the excitement you will encounter inside. The foyer passes the formal dining room on the way to the columned gallery. The formal living room opens to the rear patio and has easy access to a wet bar. The contemporary kitchen has a work island and all the amenities for gourmet preparation. The family room will be a favorite for casual entertainment. The family sleeping wing begins with an octagonal vestibule and has three bedrooms with private baths. The master wing features a private garden and an opulent bath.

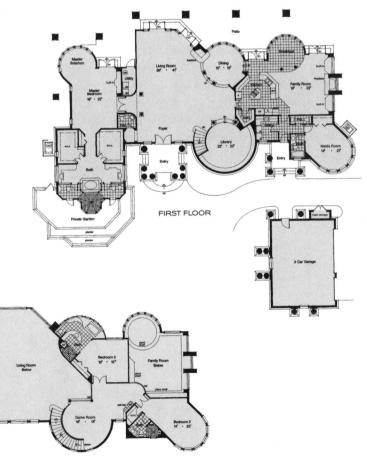

plan # HPT7600107

Style: Mediterranean
First Floor: 4,284 sq. ft.
Second Floor: 1,319 sq. ft.
Total: 5,603 sq. ft.
Bedrooms: 4
Bathrooms: 4½ + ½
Width: 109' - 4"
Depth: 73' - 2"
Foundation: Slab

SEARCH ONLINE @ EPLANS.COM

A hint of Moroccan architecture, with columns, arches, and walls of glass, makes an arresting appearance in this home. It allows a diverse arrangement of space inside, for a dynamic floor plan. The foyer spills openly into the immense living area and sunken dining room. A stair encircles the sunken library/great space for a home theater. Beyond is the family room with a two-story high media wall and built-ins, plus the circular breakfast room and island kitchen. A maid's room, or guest room, has a full circular wall of glass and leads to the garage through a covered entry and drive-through area. The master suite is true luxury: circular sitting area, His and Hers facilities, and a private garden. Upstairs is a game room, plus two family bedrooms with private amenity-filled baths.

FIRST FLOOR

SECOND FLOOR

Chic and glamorous, this Mediterranean facade pairs ancient shapes, such as square columns, with a refined disposition set off by radius windows. A magnificent entry leads to an interior gallery and the great room. This extraordinary space is warmed by a two-sided fireplace and defined by extended views of the rear property. Sliding glass doors to a wraparound veranda create great indoor/outdoor flow. The gourmet kitchen easily serves any occasion and provides a pass-through to the outdoor kitchen. A powder room accommodates visitors, and an elevator leads to the sleeping quarters upstairs. Double doors open to the master suite, which features a walk-in closet, two-sided fireplace, and angled whirlpool bath. The master bedroom boasts a tray ceiling and doors to a spacious deck. The upper-level catwalk leads to a bedroom suite that can easily accommodate a guest or live-in relative. The basement level features future space and a two-car garage.

plan # HPT7600108

Style: Italianate
First Floor: 2,491 sq. ft.
Second Floor: 1,290 sq. ft.
Total: 3,781 sq. ft.
Bonus Space: 358 sq. ft.
Bedrooms: 5
Bathrooms: 4½
Width: 62' - 0"
Depth: 67' - 0"
Foundation: Basement

SEARCH ONLINE @ EPLANS.COM

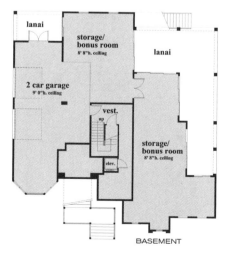

BASEMENT

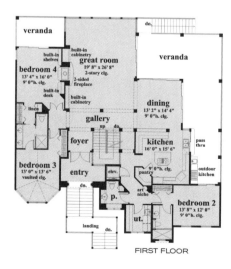

FIRST FLOOR

SECOND FLOOR

ORDER BLUEPRINTS 24 HOURS, 7 DAYS A WEEK, AT 1-800-521-6797

© The Sater Design Collection, Inc.

plan# HPT7600109

Style: Italianate
First Floor: 1,995 sq. ft.
Second Floor: 2,165 sq. ft.
Total: 4,160 sq. ft.
Bedrooms: 5
Bathrooms: 5½
Width: 58' - 0"
Depth: 65' - 0"
Foundation: Slab

SEARCH ONLINE @ EPLANS.COM

With a Spanish tile roof and Italian Renaissance detailing, this estate home holds the best of the Mediterranean. Upon entry, the foyer opens up to the living room/dining room combination, a highly requested feature in today's homes. A two-sided fireplace here shares its warmth with the study/library. The gourmet kitchen maximizes work space with wraparound countertops and an oversize island. The leisure room will be a family favorite, with a built-in entertainment center and outdoor access. Don't miss the outdoor grill and cabana suite on the far right. The master retreat is aptly named; a unique shape allows for an angled bath with a whirlpool tub and twin walk-in closets. Three additional bedrooms with private baths share two sunporches and convenient utility space.

FIRST FLOOR

SECOND FLOOR

© The Sater Design Collection, Inc.

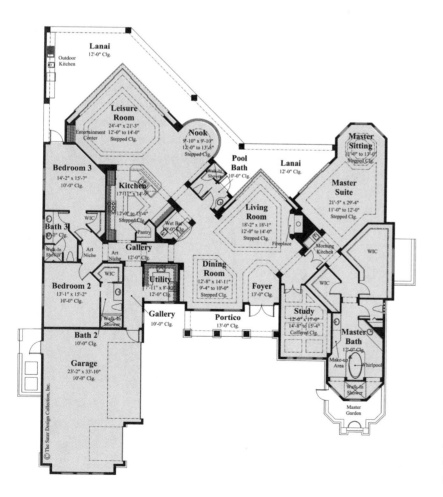

plan# HPT7600110

Style: Italianate
Square Footage: 3,942
Bedrooms: 3
Bathrooms: 4
Width: 83' - 10"
Depth: 106' - 0"
Foundation: Slab

SEARCH ONLINE @ EPLANS.COM

This sprawling Italian ranch house will surprise you at every turn. The foyer opens to the living and dining rooms, each defined by an elegant ceiling treatment. A corner fireplace in the living room offers warmth, and an angled wall of windows presents uninhibited views of the rear property. Pass the wet bar and the pool bath to enter the angled kitchen, breakfast nook set in a half-moon bow, and diamond-shaped leisure room with fantastic views. On the lanai, an outdoor kitchen invites alfresco dining. The entire right wing is devoted to the master suite. A bayed sitting area and morning kitchen are everyday luxuries—of special note are the walk-in shower and indulgent whirlpool tub set in a turret. A master garden completes this opulent escape.

ORDER BLUEPRINTS 24 HOURS, 7 DAYS A WEEK, AT 1-800-521-6797

Grand Estates

© The Sater Design Collection, Inc.

plan # HPT7600111

Style: Mediterranean
Square Footage: 3,640
Bedrooms: 3
Bathrooms: 3½
Width: 106' - 4"
Depth: 102' - 4"
Foundation: Slab

SEARCH ONLINE @ EPLANS.COM

An elegant columned entry provides a fine welcome to this home. The expansive foyer introduces the formal rooms—the study and living room, which share a fireplace, and the dining room, which opens to the rear veranda. The less-formal leisure room, with a fireplace and access to a side veranda, resides to the rear of the plan. Entertain guests in style with two luxurious guest suites that are conveniently near the living spaces; each suite features a walk-in closet and a private bath. The master suite, located to the left of the plan, boasts sliding glass doors that open to the veranda.

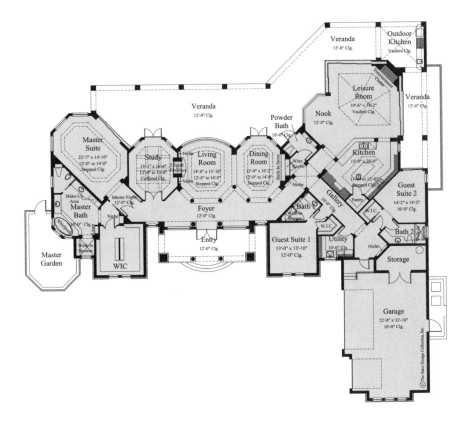

Finished with French Country adornments, this estate home is comfortable in just about any setting. Main living areas are sunk down just a bit from the entry foyer, providing them with soaring ceilings and sweeping views. The family room features a focal fireplace. A columned entry gains access to the master suite where separate sitting and sleeping areas are defined by a three-sided fireplace. There are three bedrooms upstairs; one has a private bath. The sunken media room on this level includes storage space. Look for the decks on the second level.

plan# HPT7600112

Style: French
First Floor: 2,899 sq. ft.
Second Floor: 1,472 sq. ft.
Total: 4,371 sq. ft.
Bedrooms: 4
Bathrooms: 3½ + ½
Width: 69' - 4"
Depth: 76' - 8"
Foundation: Slab

SEARCH ONLINE @ EPLANS.COM

FIRST FLOOR

SECOND FLOOR

HIDDEN SECOND
HALF BATH

ORDER BLUEPRINTS 24 HOURS, 7 DAYS A WEEK, AT 1-800-521-6797

Grand Estates

plan# HPT7600113

Style: French
First Floor: 1,729 sq. ft.
Second Floor: 2,312 sq. ft.
Total: 4,041 sq. ft.
Bedrooms: 4
Bathrooms: 3½
Width: 71' - 6"
Depth: 60' - 0"
Foundation: Crawlspace

SEARCH ONLINE @ EPLANS.COM

Entertaining will be a breeze for the owners of this imposing French manor home. Formal rooms open directly off the foyer, with a powder room nearby. Family members and friends may prefer the beam-ceilinged gathering room, with its fireplace and access to the covered front terrace. The kitchen, which easily serves both areas, features a walk-in pantry, an island cooktop and a large breakfast nook. Upstairs, the master suite contains a sitting room and access to a private balcony, as well as a sumptuous bath. A reading area is centrally located for all four bedrooms, and a recreation room adds another opportunity for relaxation.

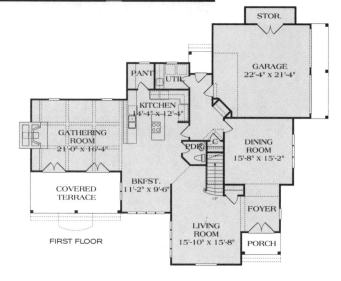

ORDER BLUEPRINTS 24 HOURS, 7 DAYS A WEEK, AT 1-800-521-6797

FIRST FLOOR

SECOND FLOOR

Here's an upscale multilevel plan with expansive rear views. The first floor provides an open living and dining area, defined by decorative columns and enhanced by natural light from tall windows. A breakfast area with a lovely triple window opens to a sunroom, which allows light to pour into the gourmet kitchen. The master wing features a tray ceiling in the bedroom, two walk-in closets, and an elegant private vestibule leading to a lavish bath. Upstairs, a reading loft overlooks the great room and leads to a sleeping area with two suites. A recreation room, exercise room, office, guest suite, and additional storage are available in the finished basement.

plan# HPT7600114

Style: Mediterranean
Main Level: 2,391 sq. ft.
Upper Level: 922 sq. ft.
Lower Level: 1,964 sq. ft.
Total: 5,277 sq. ft.
Bonus Space: 400 sq. ft.
Bedrooms: 4
Bathrooms: 4½
Width: 63' - 10"
Depth: 85' - 6"
Foundation: Basement

SEARCH ONLINE @ EPLANS.COM

LOWER LEVEL

MAIN LEVEL

UPPER LEVEL

plan # HPT7600115

Style: Mediterranean
First Floor: 2,710 sq. ft.
Second Floor: 2,784 sq. ft.
Total: 5,494 sq. ft.
Bedrooms: 3
Bathrooms: 4½
Width: 79' - 4"
Depth: 76' - 8"
Foundation: Basement

SEARCH ONLINE | @ EPLANS.COM

This Mediterranean estate features palatial elegance with all the comfortable amenities of the modern world. Double doors welcome you inside to a sunlit gallery that introduces a beautiful double staircase. The island kitchen easily serves the formal dining room. A bayed den accesses a rear deck. The gathering room is served by a bar area and is warmed by a fireplace. The study is a quiet retreat accessing a covered porch that extends to an outdoor deck. The second floor offers a plush master suite that includes a sitting area, two walk-in closets, and a private bath. Two additional suites and a playroom also reside here. The basement level is an impressive entertainment center that provides a recreation room served by a wet bar, a billiard room, home theater, gym, in-door spa, sauna, guest suite, second kitchen, and a mechanical/storage room. An elevator provides easy access to all levels.

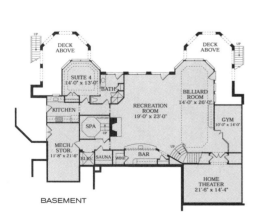

BASEMENT

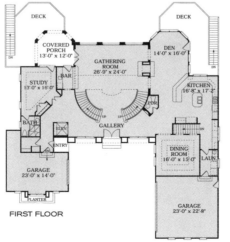

FIRST FLOOR

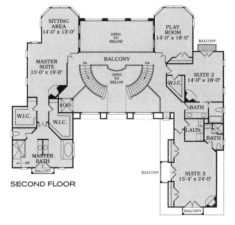

SECOND FLOOR

This exquisite home is definitely Mediterranean, with its corner quoins, lintels, and tall entry. This home features a dining room, a massive family room with a fireplace, a gourmet kitchen with a breakfast area, and a laundry room. Finishing the first floor is a lavish master suite, which enjoys a vast walk-in closet, a sitting area, and a pampering private bath. The finished basement features three suites, two full baths, a pool room, and a recreation room/theater along with two storage rooms.

plan# HPT7600116

Style: Mediterranean
Main Level: 2,262 sq. ft.
Lower Level: 1,822 sq. ft.
Total: 4,084 sq. ft.
Bedrooms: 4
Bathrooms: 3½
Width: 109' - 11"
Depth: 46' - 0"
Foundation: Basement

SEARCH ONLINE @ EPLANS.COM

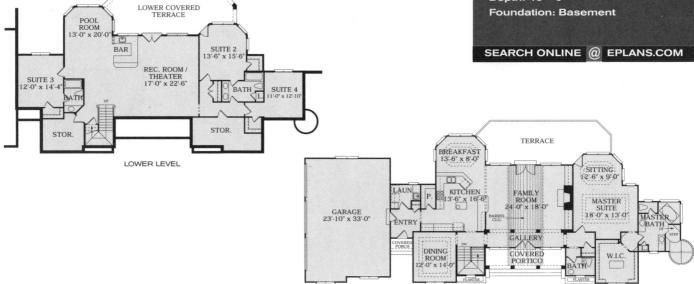

LOWER LEVEL

MAIN LEVEL

plan# HPT7600117

Style: Mediterranean
First Floor: 3,300 sq. ft.
Second Floor: 1,973 sq. ft.
Total: 5,273 sq. ft.
Bonus Space: 960 sq. ft.
Bedrooms: 4
Bathrooms: 5½
Width: 107' - 10"
Depth: 75' - 7"
Foundation: Basement

SEARCH ONLINE @ EPLANS.COM

This exciting Mediterranean villa is a lavish design filled with a modern array of amenities. A portico welcomes you inside, where formal rooms offer breathtaking interior vistas. The casual areas of the home include a gourmet island kitchen, breakfast room and family room warmed by a fireplace. The first-floor master suite provides a sitting bay, private bath, and two walk-in closets. Three additional family suites reside upstairs, along with an office/suite and spacious recreation room. The basement level is reserved for entertainment, starting with a pool room served by a bar, a sitting room with a fireplace, a media room, an exercise room with a sauna, a guest suite, and mechanical/storage room. The elevator is a convenient touch.

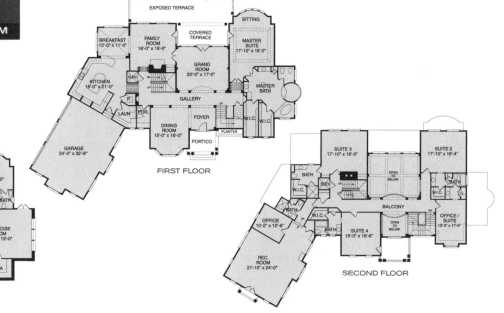

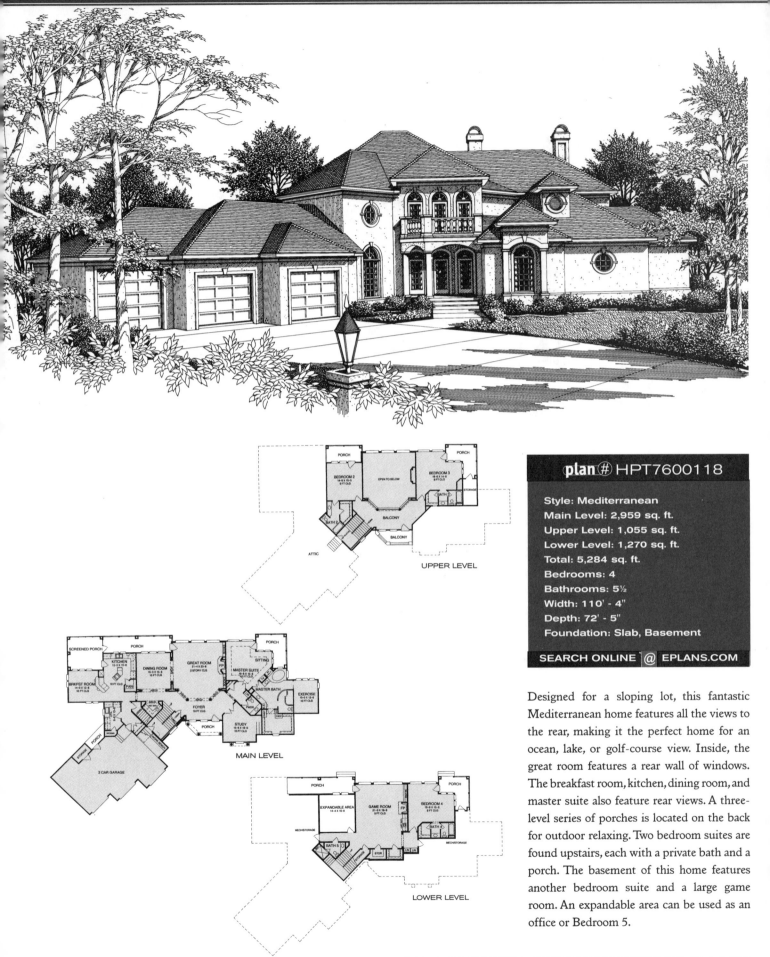

PORCH

BEDROOM 2
14-6 X 15-0
9-FT CLG

OPEN TO BELOW

BEDROOM 3
15-6 X 14-6
9-FT CLG

PORCH

BATH

STORAGE

BATH 2

BALCONY

BALCONY

ATTIC

UPPER LEVEL

SCREENED PORCH

PORCH

KITCHEN
13-0 X 15-6

DINING ROOM
15-0 X 13-6
10-FT CLG

GREAT ROOM
21-4 X 20-6
2 STORY CLG

SITTING

PORCH

FP

MASTER SUITE
16-6 X 15-6
9-FT CLG

PAN

BRKFST ROOM
14-0 X 12-6
10-FT CLG

MASTER BATH

EXERCISE
15-0 X 13-6
10-FT CLG

FOYER
10-FT CLG

STUDY
15-4 X 16-6
10-FT CLG

PORCH

PORCH

STORAGE

3 CAR GARAGE

MAIN LEVEL

PORCH

EXPANDABLE AREA
14-6 X 15-0

GAME ROOM
21-4 X 19-6
9-FT CLG

FP

BEDROOM 4
15-6 X 15-6
9-FT CLG

PORCH

MECH/STORAGE

MECH/STORAGE

BATH 5

STOR

BATH

LOWER LEVEL

plan# HPT7600118

Style: Mediterranean
Main Level: 2,959 sq. ft.
Upper Level: 1,055 sq. ft.
Lower Level: 1,270 sq. ft.
Total: 5,284 sq. ft.
Bedrooms: 4
Bathrooms: 5½
Width: 110' - 4"
Depth: 72' - 5"
Foundation: Slab, Basement

SEARCH ONLINE @ EPLANS.COM

Designed for a sloping lot, this fantastic Mediterranean home features all the views to the rear, making it the perfect home for an ocean, lake, or golf-course view. Inside, the great room features a rear wall of windows. The breakfast room, kitchen, dining room, and master suite also feature rear views. A three-level series of porches is located on the back for outdoor relaxing. Two bedroom suites are found upstairs, each with a private bath and a porch. The basement of this home features another bedroom suite and a large game room. An expandable area can be used as an office or Bedroom 5.

ORDER BLUEPRINTS 24 HOURS, 7 DAYS A WEEK, AT 1-800-521-6797

plan # HPT7600119

Style: Mediterranean
First Floor: 3,264 sq. ft.
Second Floor: 1,671 sq. ft.
Total: 4,935 sq. ft.
Bedrooms: 4
Bathrooms: 3½
Width: 96' - 10"
Depth: 65' - 1"
Foundation: Slab, Crawlspace

SEARCH ONLINE @ EPLANS.COM

A very efficient plan that minimizes the use of enclosed hallways creates a very open feeling of space and orderliness. As you enter the foyer you have a clear view through the spacious living room to the covered patio beyond. The formal dining area is to the right and the master wing is to the left. The master bedroom boasts a sitting area, access to the patio, His and Hers walk-in closets, dual vanities, a walk-in shower, and a compartmented toilet. A large island kitchen overlooks the nook and family room, which has a built-in media/fireplace wall. Three additional bedrooms and two full baths complete the plan.

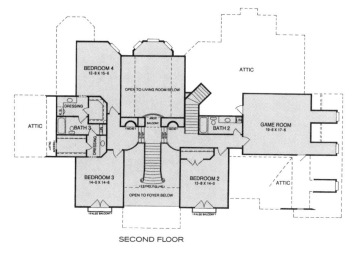

SECOND FLOOR

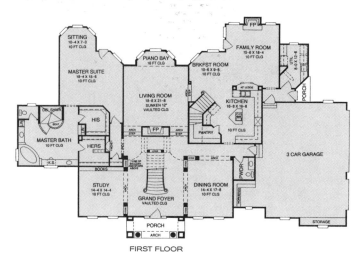

FIRST FLOOR

Grand Estates

Making a grand entrance is almost required with this fine two-story stucco home. The elegant loggia leads to the foyer where a beam-ceilinged study waits on the right. Directly ahead is a wonderfully large living room, complete with a warming fireplace, built-ins, and access to the rear veranda. A spacious formal dining room also offers access to the veranda and is easily serviced by the large island kitchen. Note the studio with a built-in darkroom at the front of the home. The deluxe master suite is designed to pamper. Upstairs, two suites offer private baths and walk-in closets. A game/TV room is enhanced by a third fireplace and sits adjacent to a sewing room. There are two large unfinished rooms completing this floor.

plan# HPT7600120

Style: Mediterranean
First Floor: 3,562 sq. ft.
Second Floor: 1,366 sq. ft.
Total: 4,928 sq. ft.
Bonus Space: 957 sq. ft.
Bedrooms: 3
Bathrooms: 3½
Width: 134' - 8"
Depth: 89' - 8"
Foundation: Crawlspace

SEARCH ONLINE @ EPLANS.COM

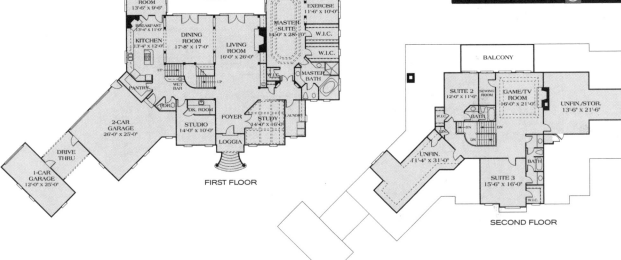

FIRST FLOOR

SECOND FLOOR

ORDER BLUEPRINTS 24 HOURS, 7 DAYS A WEEK, AT 1-800-521-6797

A distinctively French flair is the hallmark of this European design. Inside, the two-story foyer provides views to the huge great room beyond. A well-placed study off the foyer provides space for a home office. The kitchen, breakfast room, and sunroom are adjacent to lend a spacious feel. The great room is visible from this area through decorative arches. The master suite includes a roomy sitting area and a lovely bath with a centerpiece whirlpool tub flanked by half-columns. Upstairs, Bedrooms 2 and 3 share a bath that includes separate dressing areas.

SECOND FLOOR

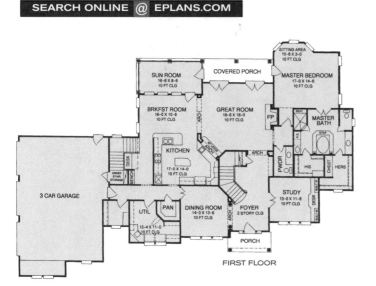

FIRST FLOOR

Details make an architectural grand gesture on the exterior of this estate home. It says, not only grand house, but great home. Living areas center in the great room and family room with attached sun space. The kitchen is defined by a low counter and an island work area. It connects to the formal dining room through a handy butler's pantry. The first-floor master suite has a sun-drenched sitting area and estate-sized bath with dual closets. For working at home, or handling family business, the secluded office is private and commodious. Four family bedrooms are all upstairs. Two have private baths; two share a Jack-and-Jill bath. A game room with a fireplace is also upstairs.

plan# HPT7600122

Style: French
First Floor: 4,145 sq. ft.
Second Floor: 2,756 sq. ft.
Total: 6,901 sq. ft.
Bedrooms: 5
Bathrooms: 4½ + ½
Width: 99' - 4"
Depth: 64' - 10"
Foundation: Slab

SEARCH ONLINE @ EPLANS.COM

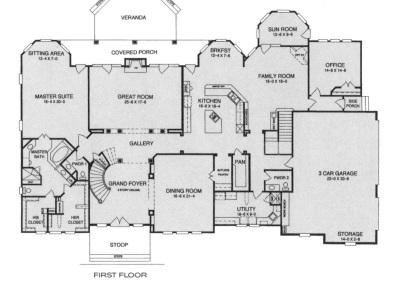

FIRST FLOOR

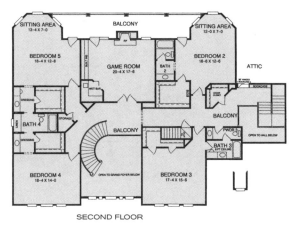

SECOND FLOOR

ORDER BLUEPRINTS 24 HOURS, 7 DAYS A WEEK, AT 1-800-521-6797

plan# HPT7600123

Style: French
First Floor: 2,870 sq. ft.
Second Floor: 2,502 sq. ft.
Total: 5,372 sq. ft.
Bedrooms: 5
Bathrooms: 5½
Width: 72' - 0"
Depth: 66' - 6"
Foundation: Crawlspace, Basement

SEARCH ONLINE @ EPLANS.COM

This lovely chateau calls to mind the lavender fields and tree-lined lanes of Southern France, but its floor plan is pure modern convenience. Fireplaces warm the living and family rooms, as well as the master bedroom. A butler's pantry connects the dining room and kitchen. Four bedrooms, including the lavish master suite, are found upstairs, and a fifth bedroom is on the first floor.

SECOND FLOOR

FIRST FLOOR

You'll be amazed at what this estate has to offer. A study/parlor and a formal dining room announce a grand foyer. Ahead, the living room offers a wet bar and French doors to the rear property. The kitchen is dazzling, with an enormous pantry, oversized cooktop island... even a pizza oven! The gathering room has a corner fireplace and accesses the covered veranda. To the far right, the master suite is a delicious retreat from the world. A bowed window lets in light and a romantic fireplace makes chilly nights cozy. The luxurious bath is awe-inspiring, with a Roman tub and separate compartmented toilet areas—one with a bidet. Upstairs, three family bedrooms share a generous bonus room. A separate pool house is available, which includes a fireplace, full bath, and dressing area.

plan# HPT7600124

Style: Mediterranean
First Floor: 3,307 sq. ft.
Second Floor: 1,642 sq. ft.
Total: 4,949 sq. ft.
Bonus Space: 373 sq. ft.
Bedrooms: 5
Bathrooms: 5½
Width: 143' - 3"
Depth: 71' - 2"
Foundation: Crawlspace

SEARCH ONLINE @ EPLANS.COM

FIRST FLOOR

SECOND FLOOR

ORDER BLUEPRINTS 24 HOURS, 7 DAYS A WEEK, AT 1-800-521-6797

Grand Estates

plan# HPT7600125

Style: Mediterranean
First Floor: 2,971 sq. ft.
Second Floor: 2,199 sq. ft.
Third Floor: 1,040 sq. ft.
Total: 6,210 sq. ft.
Bedrooms: 5
Bathrooms: 4½
Width: 84' - 4"
Depth: 64' - 11"
Foundation: Basement

SEARCH ONLINE @ EPLANS.COM

SECOND FLOOR

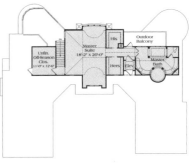

THIRD FLOOR

FIRST FLOOR

BASEMENT

Symmetry and stucco present true elegance on the facade of this five-bedroom home, and the elegance continues inside over four separate levels. Note the formal and informal gathering areas on the main level: the music room, the lake living room, the formal dining room, and the uniquely shaped breakfast room. The second level contains three large bedroom suites—one with its own bath—a spacious girl's room for play time, and an entrance room to the third-floor master suite. Lavish is the only way to describe this suite. Complete with His and Hers walk-in closets, a private balcony, an off-season closet, and a sumptuous bath, this suite is designed to pamper the homeowner. In the basement is yet more room for casual get-togethers. Note the large sitting room as well as the hobby/crafts room. And tying it all together, an elevator offers stops at each floor.

ORDER BLUEPRINTS 24 HOURS, 7 DAYS A WEEK, AT 1-800-521-6797

Mediterranean Inspiration 165

This home features a spectacular blend of arch-top windows, French doors, and balusters. An impressive informal leisure room has a 16-foot tray ceiling, an entertainment center, and a grand ale bar. The large gourmet kitchen is well appointed and easily serves the nook and formal dining room. The master suite has a large bedroom and a bayed sitting area. His and Hers vanities and walk-in closets and a curved glass-block shower are highlights in the bath. The staircase leads to the deluxe secondary guest suites, two of which have observation decks to the rear and each with their own full baths.

plan # HPT7600126

Style: Mediterranean
First Floor: 4,760 sq. ft.
Second Floor: 1,552 sq. ft.
Total: 6,312 sq. ft.
Bedrooms: 5
Bathrooms: 6½
Width: 98' - 0"
Depth: 103' - 8"
Foundation: Slab

SEARCH ONLINE @ EPLANS.COM

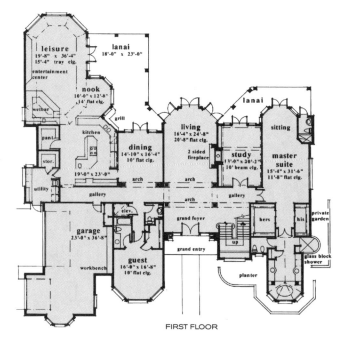

FIRST FLOOR

SECOND FLOOR

ORDER BLUEPRINTS 24 HOURS, 7 DAYS A WEEK, AT 1-800-521-6797

Grand Estates

© The Sater Group, Inc.

plan# HPT7600127

Style: Italianate
First Floor: 2,841 sq. ft.
Second Floor: 1,052 sq. ft.
Total: 3,893 sq. ft.
Bedrooms: 4
Bathrooms: 3½
Width: 85' - 0"
Depth: 76' - 8"
Foundation: Slab, Basement

SEARCH ONLINE @ EPLANS.COM

Ensure an elegant lifestyle with this luxurious plan. A turret, two-story bay windows, and plenty of arched glass impart a graceful style to the exterior, and rich amenities inside furnish contentment. A grand foyer decked with columns introduces the living room with curved-glass windows viewing the rear gardens. The study and living room share a through-fireplace. The master suite enjoys a tray ceiling, two walk-in closets, a separate shower, and a garden tub set in a bay window. Informal entertainment will be a breeze with a rich leisure room adjoining the kitchen and breakfast nook and opening to a rear veranda. Upstairs, two family bedrooms and a guest suite with a private deck complete the plan.

SECOND FLOOR

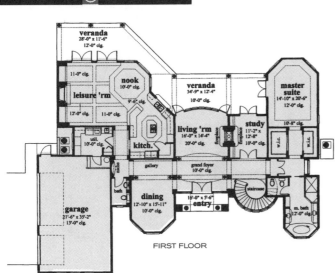

FIRST FLOOR

© The Sater Design Collection, Inc.

An impressive Italian Renaissance manor, this stone-and-stucco home is stunning from the curb and pure rapture inside. Twin bays at the front of the plan hold a study with a star-stepped ceiling and a dining room with coffer accents and decorative columns. The great room offers a warming fireplace and a soaring coffered ceiling. Not to be missed: an outdoor kitchen in addition to the modern country kitchen and bayed breakfast nook inside. The master suite is a dream come true; a large bay window, oversize walk-in closets, and a pampering bath with a corner tub will delight. Upstairs, three bedrooms all have private baths and large walk-in closets. Two bedrooms enjoy deck access.

plan# HPT7600128

Style: French
First Floor: 2,232 sq. ft.
Second Floor: 1,269 sq. ft.
Total: 3,501 sq. ft.
Bedrooms: 4
Bathrooms: 4½
Width: 63' - 9"
Depth: 80' - 0"
Foundation: Slab

SEARCH ONLINE @ EPLANS.COM

FIRST FLOOR

SECOND FLOOR

ORDER BLUEPRINTS 24 HOURS, 7 DAYS A WEEK, AT 1-800-521-6797

© The Sater Design Collection, Inc.

plan # HPT7600129

Style: Mediterranean
First Floor: 2,815 sq. ft.
Second Floor: 1,130 sq. ft.
Total: 3,945 sq. ft.
Bedrooms: 4
Bathrooms: 3½
Width: 85' - 0"
Depth: 76' - 8"
Foundation: Slab

SEARCH ONLINE @ EPLANS.COM

Stone, stucco, beautiful windows, and a tile roof all combine to give this home plenty of classy curb appeal. An elegant entry leads to the grand foyer, which introduces the formal living room. Here, a bowed wall of windows shows off the rear veranda, and a two-sided fireplace warms cool evenings. A cozy study shares the fireplace and offers access to the rear veranda. Providing privacy as well as pampering, the first-floor master suite is complete with two walk-in closets, a deluxe bath, a stepped ceiling, and private access outdoors. For casual times, the leisure room features a fireplace, built-ins, a coffered ceiling, and outdoor access. Upstairs, Bedrooms 2 and 3 share a bath; the guest suite has a private bath.

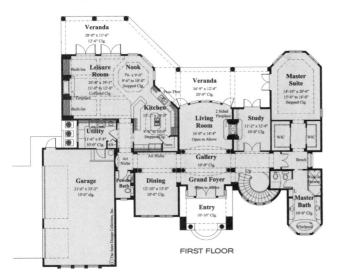

FIRST FLOOR

SECOND FLOOR

Grand Estates

Multiple rooflines and a stucco exterior establish the Spanish character of this plan. Inside, rooms are filled with lavish amenities. The family room boasts a built-in entertainment center, a fireplace, and easy access to the spacious kitchen and eating area. The nearby study features a coffered ceiling, and just off the dining room is a wine storage room. A covered rear loggia offers space to enjoy the outdoors. Upstairs, three bedrooms—all with private baths, easily access a large game/TV room.

plan# HPT7600130

Style: Spanish
First Floor: 3,148 sq. ft.
Second Floor: 2,055 sq. ft.
Total: 5,203 sq. ft.
Bedrooms: 4
Bathrooms: 4½
Width: 75' - 4"
Depth: 73' - 9"

SEARCH ONLINE @ EPLANS.COM

FIRST FLOOR

SECOND FLOOR

ORDER BLUEPRINTS 24 HOURS, 7 DAYS A WEEK, AT 1-800-521-6797

plan # HPT7600131

Style: Spanish
First Floor: 3,103 sq. ft.
Second Floor: 1,616 sq. ft.
Total: 4,719 sq. ft.
Bedrooms: 4
Bathrooms: 3½ + ½
Width: 86' - 9"
Depth: 84' - 6"

SEARCH ONLINE @ EPLANS.COM

This stunning manor is rich with Spanish character. The interior is highlighted by unusually shaped rooms, elegant ceiling treatments, and an expansive loggia with an outdoor kitchen. Four bedrooms—including a resplendent master suite—all provide relaxing sanctuaries. A large game room, with access to a balcony, is the highlight of the second floor.

SECOND FLOOR

FIRST FLOOR

BASEMENT STAIR LOCATION

An elegant front porch, columns inside and out, various ceiling treatments, and decorative windows create a spectacular home. An open floor plan provides large formal and informal spaces. The island kitchen with extensive counter space offers easy access to the formal dining and breakfast areas. Located for privacy, the impressive master bedroom suite showcases a deluxe dressing room with a whirlpool tub, dual vanities, an oversized shower, and a walk-in closet. A library is located near the master bedroom. Split stairs are positioned for family convenience and lead to three bedrooms, each with large walk-in closets and private access to a bath. A three-car garage and full basement complete this exciting showplace.

plan # HPT7600132

Style: French
First Floor: 3,087 sq. ft.
Second Floor: 1,037 sq. ft.
Total: 4,124 sq. ft.
Bedrooms: 4
Bathrooms: 3½
Width: 92' - 2"
Depth: 70' - 10"
Foundation: Basement

SEARCH ONLINE @ EPLANS.COM

FIRST FLOOR

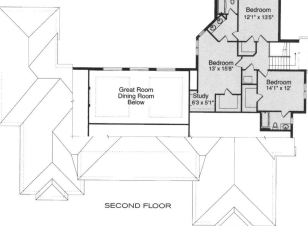

SECOND FLOOR

plan# HPT7600133

Style: Mediterranean
First Floor: 3,323 sq. ft.
Second Floor: 1,820 sq. ft.
Total: 5,143 sq. ft.
Bedrooms: 4
Bathrooms: 3½
Width: 113' - 10"
Depth: 60' - 6"
Foundation: Basement

SEARCH ONLINE @ EPLANS.COM

In exquisite Italian Renaissance style, this gracious estate uses open spaces and luxurious amenities to create a comfortable home. Enter under an impressive covered courtyard to the grand foyer; the elegant dining room and stately library lie to either side. Ahead, a professional-grade kitchen is equipped with a cooktop island and opens to central informal dining. The great room features a warming fireplace and access to the rear deck. The first-floor master suite celebrates luxury with a lavish bath, sunlit sitting area, and room-sized closet. Two generous bedrooms and a full guest suite share the upper level. The lower level can be finished to accommodate media and exercise rooms, a sitting area, and wine storage.

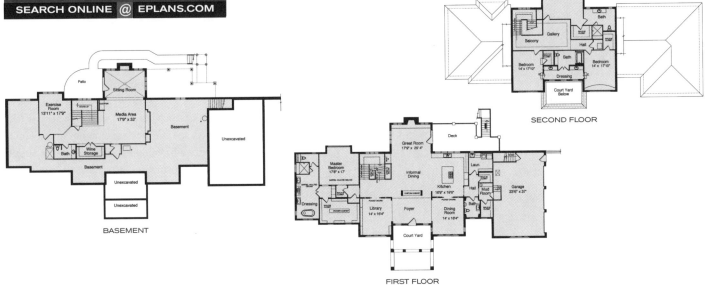

BASEMENT

SECOND FLOOR

FIRST FLOOR

Grand Estates

SECOND FLOOR

- MOTHER IN-LAW SUITE 12'-8" x 25'-6"
- REC. ROOM 20'-0" x 15'-8"
- SUITE 5 15'-0" x 13'-0"
- SUITE 4 15'-4" x 12'-6"
- BATH
- W.I.C.
- SUITE 2 14'-4" x 17'-0"
- SUITE 3 14'-6" x 17'-0"

FIRST FLOOR

- VERANDA
- BREAKFAST 15'-0" x 10'-6"
- FAMILY ROOM 22'-0" x 16'-6"
- GARAGE 23'-6" x 32'-6"
- KITCHEN 15'-0" x 14'-0"
- PDR
- LAUN
- DINING ROOM 15'-0" x 15'-6"
- LIVING ROOM 25'-0" x 17'-0"
- MASTER BATH
- FOYER
- MASTER SUITE 18'-0" x 17'-0"
- W.I.C.
- STOOP

plan # HPT7600134

Style: French
First Floor: 2,446 sq. ft.
Second Floor: 1,988 sq. ft.
Total: 4,434 sq. ft.
Bonus Space: 651 sq. ft.
Bedrooms: 5
Bathrooms: 4½
Width: 61' - 2"
Depth: 78' - 10"
Foundation: Crawlspace

SEARCH ONLINE @ EPLANS.COM

Here is a home with Old World charm and the perfect footprint for a narrow lot. Decorative balustrades, vertical shutters and arches add nice finishing touches to the brick exterior. Inside, 11-foot ceilings give added spaciousness throughout the first floor. The front stoop leads to a small foyer, then to the formal living room. A second fireplace is found in the family room, which is separated by columned arches from the breakfast area and the island kitchen. A wall of French doors brightens this area and opens to a veranda stretching across the back of the house. The master suite, at the front, pampers with a large walk-in closet, dual vanities, and a garden tub. Family members and guests will appreciate the second-floor sleeping quarters and recreation room.

ORDER BLUEPRINTS 24 HOURS, 7 DAYS A WEEK, AT 1-800-521-6797

Grand Estates

plan# HPT7600135

Style: French
First Floor: 2,272 sq. ft.
Second Floor: 1,154 sq. ft.
Total: 3,426 sq. ft.
Bonus Space: 513 sq. ft.
Bedrooms: 4
Bathrooms: 3½
Width: 102' - 8"
Depth: 49' - 6"
Foundation: Crawlspace, Basement

SEARCH ONLINE @ EPLANS.COM

The gracious facade of this French home engages refinement and fantasy. The foyer is housed within the turret, which holds an elegant spiral staircase. To the left, gourmet entertaining can be had with the spacious island kitchen that serves both the casual breakfast room and the formal dining room. Enjoy a nightcap in front of a relaxing fire in the great room. With comfort in mind, the master suite features a fireplace and a sumptuous bath. The upper floor creates a space for guests and family members with three secondary bedrooms—one with a private bath—and a future recreation room.

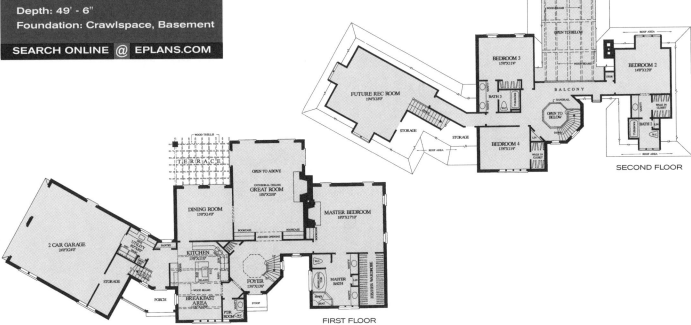

SECOND FLOOR

FIRST FLOOR

The design of this French Country estate captures its ambiance with its verandas, grand entry, and unique balconies. A spectacular panorama of the formal living areas and the elegant curved stairway awaits just off the foyer. A large island kitchen, breakfast nook, and family room will impress, as will the wine cellar. Plenty of kitchen pantry space leads to the laundry and motor court featuring a two-car garage attached to the main house and a three-car garage attached by a breezeway. The master suite boasts a sunken sitting area with a see-through fireplace, His and Hers walk-in closets, island tub, and large separate shower. A study area, three additional bedrooms, a full bath, and a bonus area reside on the second floor.

plan # HPT7600136

Style: French Country
First Floor: 3,517 sq. ft.
Second Floor: 1,254 sq. ft.
Total: 4,771 sq. ft.
Bedrooms: 5
Bathrooms: 4½ + ½
Width: 95' - 8"
Depth: 107' - 0"
Foundation: Slab

SEARCH ONLINE @ EPLANS.COM

FIRST FLOOR

SECOND FLOOR

ORDER BLUEPRINTS 24 HOURS, 7 DAYS A WEEK, AT 1-800-521-6797

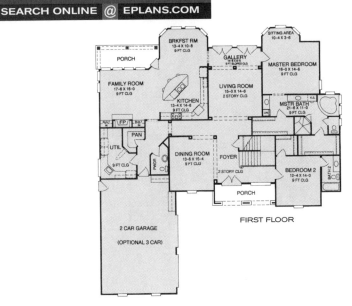

FIRST FLOOR

PORCH

BRKFST RM
13-4 X 10-8
9 FT CLG

FAMILY ROOM
17-6 X 16-0
9 FT CLG

GALLERY
14-8 X 8-0
9 FT SLOPED CLG

SITTING AREA
10-4 X 3-6

MASTER BEDROOM
16-0 X 14-6
9 FT CLG

KITCHEN
13-4 X 14-6
9 FT CLG

LIVING ROOM
15-0 X 14-6
2 STORY CLG

MSTR BATH
21-6 X 11-0
9 FT CLG

FP

PAN

UTIL
9 FT CLG

PWDR

DINING ROOM
13-6 X 15-4
9 FT CLG

FOYER
2 STORY CLG

BEDROOM 2
12-4 X 14-0
9 FT CLG

BATH 2

PORCH

2 CAR GARAGE
(OPTIONAL 3 CAR)

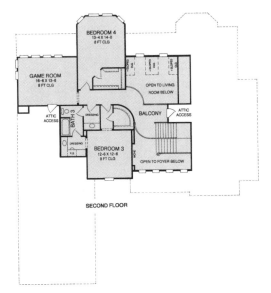

SECOND FLOOR

BEDROOM 4
13-4 X 14-0
8 FT CLG

GAME ROOM
16-6 X 13-6
8 FT CLG

OPEN TO LIVING
ROOM BELOW

ATTIC
ACCESS

BATH 3

DRESSING

BALCONY

ATTIC
ACCESS

DRESSING

BEDROOM 3
12-6 X 12-6
8 FT CLG

OPEN TO FOYER BELOW

plan# HPT7600137

Style: French Country
First Floor: 2,788 sq. ft.
Second Floor: 1,116 sq. ft.
Total: 3,904 sq. ft.
Bedrooms: 4
Bathrooms: 3½
Width: 68' - 10"
Depth: 76' - 4"
Foundation: Crawlspace, Slab, Basement

SEARCH ONLINE @ EPLANS.COM

Straight from the hills of the French countryside, this whimsical estate features every amenity on your wish list with the style and grace you've been searching for. Enter through French doors to a two-story foyer; on the left, a dining room is defined by columns. The living room is ahead, adorned with columns and leading into a gallery with rear-property access. The master suite is entered via the gallery and delights in a bayed sitting area, lavish whirlpool bath, and two generous walk-in closets. Living areas on the opposite side of the home include a kitchen with a unique serving island and a sunlit family room with a fireplace. The upper level hosts two bedrooms, a game room, and a full bath. A balcony overlook to the living room is an elegant touch.

This magnificent estate is detailed with exterior charm: a porte cochere connecting the detached garage to the house, a covered terrace, and oval windows. The first floor consists of a lavish master suite, a cozy library with a fireplace, a grand room/solarium combination, and an elegant formal dining room with another fireplace. Three bedrooms dominate the second floor—each features a walk-in closet. For the kids, there is a playroom and, upstairs, a room for future expansion into a deluxe studio with a fireplace. Over the three-car garage, there is space for a future mother-in-law or maid's suite.

plan# HPT7600138

Style: French
First Floor: 3,703 sq. ft.
Second Floor: 1,427 sq. ft.
Total: 5,130 sq. ft.
Bonus Space: 1,399 sq. ft.
Bedrooms: 4
Bathrooms: 3½ + ½
Width: 125' - 2"
Depth: 58' - 10"
Foundation: Walkout Basement

SEARCH ONLINE @ EPLANS.COM

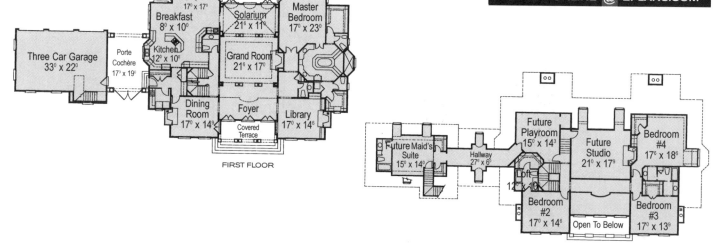

FIRST FLOOR

SECOND FLOOR

ORDER BLUEPRINTS 24 HOURS, 7 DAYS A WEEK, AT 1-800-521-6797

plan# HPT7600139

Style: Mediterranean
First Floor: 3,350 sq. ft.
Second Floor: 1,298 sq. ft.
Total: 4,648 sq. ft.
Bedrooms: 5
Bathrooms: 3½ + ½
Width: 97' - 0"
Depth: 74' - 4"
Foundation: Basement

SEARCH ONLINE @ EPLANS.COM

Reminiscent of a Mediterranean villa, this grand manor is a showstopper on the outside and a comfortable residence on the inside. An elegant receiving hall boasts a double staircase and is flanked by the formal dining room and the library. A huge gathering room at the back is graced by a fireplace and a wall of sliding glass doors to the rear terrace. The master bedroom resides on the first floor for privacy. With a lavish bath to pamper and His and Hers walk-in closets, this suite will be a delight to retire to each evening. Upstairs are four additional bedrooms with ample storage space, a large balcony overlooking the gathering room, and two full baths.

QUOTE ONE®
Cost to build? See page 187
to order complete cost estimate
to build this house in your area!

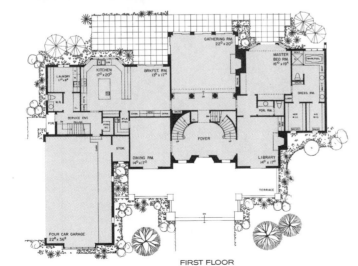

FIRST FLOOR

SECOND FLOOR

Grand Estates

The ornamental stucco detailing on this home creates an Old World charm. The two-story foyer with a sweeping curved stair opens to the large formal dining room and study. The two-story great room overlooks the rear patio. A large kitchen with an island workstation opens to an octagonal-shaped breakfast room and the family room. The master suite, offering convenient access to the study, is complete with a fireplace, two walk-in closets, and a bath with twin vanities and a separate shower and tub. A staircase located off the family room provides additional access to the three second-floor bedrooms that each offer walk-in closets and plenty of storage.

plan# HPT7600140

Style: Mediterranean
First Floor: 3,568 sq. ft.
Second Floor: 1,667 sq. ft.
Total: 5,235 sq. ft.
Bedrooms: 4
Bathrooms: 3½
Width: 86' - 8"
Depth: 79' - 0"
Foundation: Walkout Basement

SEARCH ONLINE @ EPLANS.COM

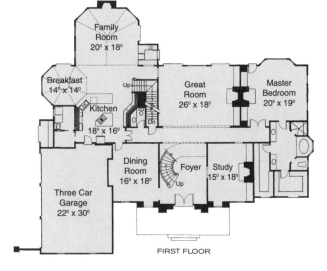

FIRST FLOOR

SECOND FLOOR

ORDER BLUEPRINTS 24 HOURS, 7 DAYS A WEEK, AT 1-800-521-6797

eplans.com

THE GATEWAY
TO YOUR NEW HOME

Looking for more plans? Got questions?
Try our one-stop home plans resource—eplans.com.

We'll help you streamline the plan selection process, so your dreams can become reality faster than you ever imagined. From choosing your home plan and ideal location to finding an experienced contractor, eplans.com will guide you every step of the way.

Mix and match! Explore! At eplans.com you can combine all your top criteria to find your perfect match. Search for your ideal home plan by any or all of the following:
> Number of bedrooms or baths,
> Total square feet,
> House style, and
> Cost.

With over 10,000 plans, the options are endless. Colonial, ranch, country, and Victorian are just a few of the house styles offered. Keep in mind your essential lifestyle features—whether to include a porch, fireplace, bonus room, or main-floor laundry room. And the garage—how many cars must it accommodate, if any? By filling out the preference page on eplans.com, we'll help you narrow your search.

At eplans.com we'll make the building process a snap to understand. At the click of a button you'll find a complete building guide. And our eplans task planner will create a construction calendar just for you. Here you'll find links to tips and other valuable information to help you every step of the way—from choosing a site to moving day.

For your added convenience, our home plans experts are available for live, one-on-one chats at eplans.com. Building a home may seem like a complicated project, but it doesn't have to be—particularly if you'll let us help you from start to finish.

COPYRIGHT DOS & DON'TS

Blueprints for residential construction (or working drawings, as they are often called in the industry) are copyrighted intellectual property, protected under the terms of United States Copyright Law and, therefore, cannot be copied legally for use in building. However, we've made it easy for you to get what you need to build your home, without violating copyright law. Following are some guidelines to help you obtain the right number of copies for your chosen blueprint design.

COPYRIGHT DO

■ Do purchase enough copies of the blueprints to satisfy building requirements. As a rule for a home or project plan, you will need a set for yourself, two or three for your builder and subcontractors, two for the local building department, and one to three for your mortgage lender. You may want to check with your local building department or your builder to see how many they need before you purchase. You may need to buy eight to 10 sets; note that some areas of the country require purchase of vellums (also called reproducibles) instead of blueprints. Vellums can be written on and changed more easily than blueprints. Also, remember, plans are only good for one-time construction.

■ Do consider reverse blueprints if you want to flop the plan. Lettering and numbering will appear backward, but the reversed sets will help you and your builder better visualize the design.

■ Do take advantage of multiple-set discounts at the time you place your order. Usually, purchasing additional sets after you receive your initial order is not as cost-effective.

■ Do take advantage of vellums. Though they are a little more expensive, they can be changed, copied, and used for one-time construction of a home. You will receive a copyright release letter with your vellums that will allow you to have them copied.

■ Do talk with one of our professional service representatives before placing your order. They can give you great advice about what packages are available for your chosen design and what will work best for your particular situation.

COPYRIGHT DON'T

■ Don't think you should purchase only one set of blueprints for a building project. One is fine if you want to study the plan closely, but will not be enough for actual building.

■ Don't expect your builder or a copy center to make copies of standard blueprints. They cannot legally—most copy centers are aware of this.

■ Don't purchase standard blueprints if you know you'll want to make changes to the plans; vellums are a better value.

■ Don't use blueprints or vellums more than one time. Additional fees apply if you want to build more than one time from a set of drawings. ■

hanley▲wood
HomePlanners
ORDERING IS EASY

HANLEY WOOD HOMEPLANNERS HAS EVERYTHING YOU NEED to build the home of your dreams, and with more than 50 years of experience in the industry, we make it as easy as possible for you to reach those goals. Just follow the steps on these pages and you'll receive a high-quality, ready-to-build set of home blueprints, plus everything else you need to make your home-building effort a success.

WHERE TO BEGIN?
1. CHOOSE YOUR PLAN

■ Browsing magazines, books, and eplans.com can be an exciting and rewarding part of the home-building process. As you search, make a list of the things you want in your dream home—everything from number of bedrooms and baths to details like fireplaces or a home office.

■ Take the time to consider your lot and your neighborhood, and how the home you choose will fit with both. And think about the future—how might your needs change if you plan to live in this house for five, 10, or 20 years?

■ With thousands of plans available, chances are that you'll have no trouble discovering your dream home. If you find something that's almost perfect, our Customization Program can help make it exactly what you want.

■ Most important, be sure to enjoy the process of picking out your new home!

WHAT YOU'LL GET WITH YOUR ORDER

Each designer's blueprint set is unique, but they all provide everything you'll need to build your home. Here are some standard elements you can expect to find in your plans:

1. FRONT PERSPECTIVE
This artist's sketch of the exterior of the house gives you an idea of how the house will look when built and landscaped.

2. FOUNDATION PLANS
This sheet shows the foundation layout including support walls, excavated and unexcavated areas, if any, and foundation notes. If your plan features slab construction rather than a basement, the plan shows footings and details for a monolithic slab. This page, or another in the set, may include a sample plot plan for locating your house on a building site.

3. DETAILED FLOOR PLANS
These plans show the layout of each floor of the house. Rooms and interior spaces are carefully dimensioned and keys are given for cross-section details provided later in the plans. The positions of electrical outlets and switches are shown.

4. HOUSE CROSS-SECTIONS
Large-scale views show sections or cutaways of the foundation, interior walls, exterior walls, floors, stairways, and roof details. Additional cross-sections may show important changes in floor, ceiling, or roof heights, or the relationship of one level to another. Extremely valuable during construction, these sections show exactly how the various parts of the house fit together.

5. INTERIOR ELEVATIONS
These elevations, or drawings, show the design and placement of kitchen and bathroom cabinets, laundry areas, fireplaces, bookcases, and other built-ins. Little extras, such as mantelpiece and wainscoting drawings, plus molding sections, provide details that give your home that custom touch.

6. EXTERIOR ELEVATIONS
Every blueprint set comes with drawings of the front exterior, and may include the rear and sides of your house as well. These drawings give necessary notes on exterior materials and finishes. Particular attention is given to cornice detail, brick, and stone accents or other finish items that make your home unique.

HANLEY WOOD HOMEPLANNERS ADVANTAGE

ORDER 24 HOURS!
1-800-521-6797

GETTING DOWN TO BUSINESS
2. PRICE YOUR PLAN

BLUEPRINT PRICE SCHEDULE

PRICE TIERS	1-SET STUDY PACKAGE	4-SET BUILDING PACKAGE	8-SET BUILDING PACKAGE	1-SET REPRODUCIBLE*
P1	$20	$50	$90	$140
P2	$40	$70	$110	$160
P3	$70	$100	$140	$190
P4	$100	$130	$170	$220
P5	$140	$170	$210	$270
P6	$180	$210	$250	$310
A1	$440	$490	$540	$660
A2	$480	$530	$580	$720
A3	$530	$590	$650	$800
A4	$575	$645	$705	$870
C1	$625	$695	$755	$935
C2	$670	$740	$800	$1000
C3	$715	$790	$855	$1075
C4	$765	$840	$905	$1150
L1	$870	$965	$1050	$1300
L2	$945	$1040	$1125	$1420
L3	$1050	$1150	$1225	$1575
L4	$1155	$1260	$1355	$1735
SQ1				.35/SQ. FT.

PRICES SUBJECT TO CHANGE

* REQUIRES A FAX NUMBER

plan
READY TO ORDER

Once you've found your plan, get your plan number and turn to the following pages to find its price tier. Use the corresponding code and the Blueprint Price Schedule above to determine your price for a variety of blueprint packages.

Keep in mind that you'll need multiple sets to fulfill building requirements, and only reproducible sets may be altered or duplicated.

To the right you'll find prices for additional and reverse blueprint sets. Also note in the following pages whether your home has a corresponding Deck or Landscape Plan, and whether you can order our Quote One® cost-to-build information or a Materials List for your plan.

IT'S EASY TO ORDER
JUST VISIT
EPLANS.COM OR CALL
TOLL-FREE
1-800-521-6797

PRICE SCHEDULE FOR ADDITIONAL OPTIONS

OPTIONS FOR PLANS IN TIERS P1-P6	COSTS
ADDITIONAL IDENTICAL BLUEPRINTS FOR "P1-P6" PLANS	$10 PER SET
REVERSE BLUEPRINTS (MIRROR IMAGE) FOR "P1-P6" PLANS	$10 FEE PER ORDER
1 SET OF DECK CONSTRUCTION DETAILS	$14.95 EACH
DECK CONSTRUCTION PACKAGE (INCLUDES 1 SET OF "P1-P6" PLANS, PLUS 1 SET STANDARD DECK CONSTRUCTION DETAILS)	ADD $10 TO BUILDING PACKAGE PRICE

OPTIONS FOR PLANS IN TIERS A1-SQ1	COSTS
ADDITIONAL IDENTICAL BLUEPRINTS IN SAME ORDER FOR "A1-L4" PLANS	$50 PER SET
REVERSE BLUEPRINTS (MIRROR IMAGE) WITH 4- OR 8-SET ORDER FOR "A1-L4" PLANS	$50 FEE PER ORDER
SPECIFICATION OUTLINES	$10 EACH
MATERIALS LISTS FOR "A1-SQ1" PLANS	$70 EACH

IMPORTANT EXTRAS	COSTS
ELECTRICAL, PLUMBING, CONSTRUCTION, AND MECHANICAL DETAIL SETS	$14.95 EACH; ANY TWO $22.95; ANY THREE $29.95; ALL FOUR $39.95
HOME FURNITURE PLANNER	$15.95 EACH
REAR ELEVATION	$10 EACH
QUOTE ONE® SUMMARY COST REPORT	$29.95
QUOTE ONE® DETAILED COST ESTIMATE (FOR MORE DETAILS ABOUT QUOTE ONE®, SEE STEP 3.)	$60

IMPORTANT NOTE
■ THE 1-SET STUDY PACKAGE IS MARKED "NOT FOR CONSTRUCTION."

Source Key
HPT76

PLAN #	PRICE TIER	PAGE	MATERIALS LIST	QUOTE ONE®	DECK	DECK PRICE	LANDSCAPE	LANDSCAPE PRICE	REGIONS
HPT7600001	SQ1	36							
HPT7600003	C4	63							
HPT7600004	L3	62							
HPT7600005	C3	130							
HPT7600007	A4	69							
HPT7600008	C1	116							
HPT7600009	SQ1	32							
HPT7600010	SQ1	44							
HPT7600011	SQ1	41							
HPT7600012	SQ1	22							
HPT7600013	SQ1	29							
HPT7600015	C2	50	Y				OLA015	P4	123568
HPT7600016	SQ1	51							
HPT7600017	SQ1	52							
HPT7600018	L1	53							
HPT7600019	C4	54							
HPT7600020	SQ1	55							
HPT7600021	SQ1	56							
HPT7600022	C3	57							
HPT7600023	C2	58							
HPT7600024	SQ1	59							
HPT7600025	C4	60							
HPT7600026	C3	61							
HPT7600027	SQ1	64							
HPT7600029	A3	66	Y						
HPT7600030	C2	67	Y						
HPT7600031	A4	68							
HPT7600032	C2	70							
HPT7600033	C1	71							
HPT7600034	C1	72							
HPT7600035	C2	73							
HPT7600036	C2	74							
HPT7600037	C2	75							
HPT7600038	A3	76	Y						
HPT7600039	A4	77	Y						
HPT7600040	A4	78	Y						
HPT7600041	C1	79	Y						
HPT7600042	C1	80							
HPT7600043	A4	81	Y						
HPT7600044	A4	82							
HPT7600045	A3	83							
HPT7600046	A4	84							
HPT7600047	A4	85							
HPT7600048	A4	86							
HPT7600049	C2	87							
HPT7600050	A3	88							
HPT7600051	C2	89							
HPT7600052	A4	90							
HPT7600053	A3	91							
HPT7600054	C1	92							
HPT7600055	A3	93							
HPT7600056	A3	94	Y						
HPT7600057	A4	95	Y						
HPT7600058	A4	96							
HPT7600060	C2	98	Y						
HPT7600061	C1	99	Y						
HPT7600062	C1	100							
HPT7600063	C1	101							
HPT7600064	C1	102							
HPT7600065	C2	103	Y	Y			OLA038	P3	7
HPT7600066	SQ1	104							
HPT7600067	C1	105							
HPT7600068	C3	106							
HPT7600069	C1	107							
HPT7600070	L1	108							
HPT7600071	C3	109							
HPT7600072	C3	110							
HPT7600073	C4	111							
HPT7600074	C3	112							
HPT7600075	C1	113							
HPT7600076	C2	114							
HPT7600077	SQ1	115							
HPT7600078	C1	117	Y						
HPT7600079	C4	118							
HPT7600080	C3	119							
HPT7600081	C3	120							
HPT7600082	C4	121							
HPT7600083	C4	122							
HPT7600084	C3	123							
HPT7600085	C3	124							
HPT7600086	C2	125							
HPT7600087	C1	126							
HPT7600088	C2	127							
HPT7600089	SQ1	128							
HPT7600090	C3	129	Y						
HPT7600091	C3	131							
HPT7600092	C4	132							
HPT7600093	C4	133							
HPT7600094	SQ1	134	Y	Y					
HPT7600095	C3	135							

PLAN #	PRICE TIER	PAGE	MATERIALS LIST	QUOTE ONE®	DECK	DECK PRICE	LANDSCAPE	LANDSCAPE PRICE	REGIONS
HPT7600096	C2	136							
HPT7600098	L2	138							
HPT7600099	SQ1	139							
HPT7600100	C3	140							
HPT7600101	SQ1	141							
HPT7600102	SQ1	142	Y						
HPT7600103	C4	143							
HPT7600104	SQ1	144							
HPT7600105	SQ1	145							
HPT7600106	SQ1	146	Y						
HPT7600107	SQ1	147							
HPT7600108	L2	148							
HPT7600109	SQ1	149							
HPT7600110	L1	150							
HPT7600111	L2	151							
HPT7600112	SQ1	152	Y						
HPT7600113	C4	153							
HPT7600114	SQ1	154	Y						
HPT7600115	SQ1	155							
HPT7600116	L2	156							
HPT7600117	SQ1	157							
HPT7600118	L1	158	Y						
HPT7600119	SQ1	159							
HPT7600120	SQ1	160							
HPT7600121	C4	161	Y						
HPT7600122	L2	162							
HPT7600123	L3	163							
HPT7600124	SQ1	164	Y						
HPT7600125	SQ1	165							
HPT7600126	SQ1	166	Y	Y		OLA008	P4	1234568	
HPT7600127	SQ1	167							
HPT7600128	L1	168							
HPT7600129	L1	169							
HPT7600130	L1	170							
HPT7600131	C4	171							
HPT7600132	C4	172							
HPT7600133	SQ1	173							
HPT7600134	C4	174							
HPT7600135	C4	175							
HPT7600136	SQ1	176							
HPT7600137	C3	177							
HPT7600138	SQ1	178	Y						
HPT7600139	L1	179	Y	Y					
HPT7600140	SQ1	180							

MORE TOOLS FOR SUCCESS
3. GET GREAT EXTRAS

WE OFFER A VARIETY OF USEFUL TOOLS THAT CAN HELP YOU THROUGH EVERY STEP OF THE home-building process. From our Materials List to our Customization Program, these items let you put our experience to work for you to ensure that you get exactly what you want out of your dream house.

MATERIALS LIST

For many of the designs in our portfolio, we offer a customized list of materials that helps you plan and estimate the cost of your new home. The Materials List outlines the quantity, type, and size of materials needed to build your house (with the exception of mechanical system items). Included are framing lumber, windows and doors, kitchen and bath cabinetry, rough and finished hardware, and much more. This handy list helps you or your builder cost out materials and serves as a reference sheet when you're compiling bids.

SPECIFICATION OUTLINE

This valuable 16-page document can play an important role in the construction of your house. Fill it in with your builder, and you'll have a step-by-step chronicle of 166 stages or items crucial to the building process. It provides a comprehensive review of the construction process and helps you choose materials.

QUOTE ONE®

The Quote One® system, which helps estimate the cost of building select designs in your zip code, is available in two parts: the Summary Cost Report and the Material Cost Report.

The Summary Cost Report, the first element in the package, breaks down the cost of your home into various categories based on building materials, labor, and installation, and includes three grades of construction: Budget, Standard, and Custom. Make even more informed decisions about your project with the second element of our package, the Material Cost Report. The material and installation cost is shown for each of more than 1,000 line items provided in the standard-grade Materials List, which is included with this tool. Additional space is included for estimates from contractors and subcontractors, such as for mechanical materials, which are not included in our packages.

If you are interested in a plan that does not indicate the availability of Quote One®, please call and ask our sales representatives, who can verify the status for you.

CUSTOMIZATION PROGRAM

If the plan you love needs something changed to make it perfect, our customization experts will ensure that you get nothing less than your dream home. Purchase a reproducible set of plans for the home you choose, and we'll send you our easy-to-use customization request form via e-mail or fax. For just $50, our customization experts will provide an estimate for your requested revisions, and once it's approved, that charge will be applied to your changes. You'll receive either five sets or a reproducible master of your modified design and any other options you select.

BUILDING BASICS

If you want to know more about building techniques—and deal more confidently with your subcontractors—we offer four useful detail sheets. These sheets provide non-plan-specific general information, but are excellent tools that will add to your understanding of Plumbing Details, Electrical Details, Construction Details, and Mechanical Details. These fact-filled sheets will help answer many of your building questions, and help you learn what questions to ask your builder and subcontractors.

HANLEY WOOD HOMEPLANNERS ADVANTAGE

ORDER 24 HOURS!
1-800-521-6797

HANDS-ON HOME FURNITURE PLANNER

Effectively plan the space in your home using our Hands-On Home Furniture Planner. It's fun and easy—no more moving heavy pieces of furniture to see how the room will go together. The kit includes reusable peel-and-stick furniture templates that fit on a 12"x18" laminated layout board—enough space to lay out every room in your house.

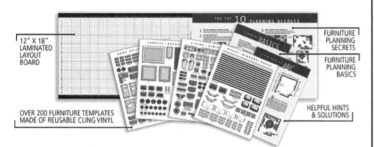

12" X 18" LAMINATED LAYOUT BOARD

FURNITURE PLANNING SECRETS

FURNITURE PLANNING BASICS

HELPFUL HINTS & SOLUTIONS

OVER 200 FURNITURE TEMPLATES MADE OF REUSABLE CLING VINYL

DECK BLUEPRINT PACKAGE

Many of the homes in this book can be enhanced with a professionally designed Home Planners Deck Plan. Those plans marked with a **D** have a corresponding deck plan, sold separately, which includes a Deck Plan Frontal Sheet, Deck Framing and Floor Plans, Deck Elevations, and a Deck Materials List. A Standard Deck Details Package, also available, provides all the how-to information necessary for building any deck. Get both the Deck Plan and the Standard Deck Details Package for one low price in our Complete Deck Building Package.

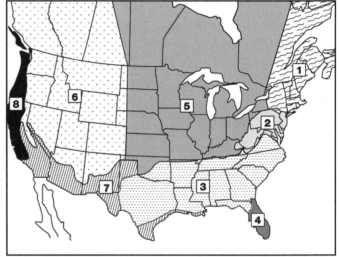

LANDSCAPE BLUEPRINT PACKAGE

Homes marked with an **L** in this book have a front-yard Landscape Plan that is complementary in design to the house plan. These comprehensive Landscape Blueprint Packages include a Frontal Sheet, Plan View, Regionalized Plant & Materials List, a sheet on Planting and Maintaining Your Landscape, Zone Maps, and a Plant Size and Description Guide. Each set of blueprints is a full 18" x 24" with clear, complete instructions in easy-to-read type.

Our Landscape Plans are available with a Plant & Materials List adapted by horticultural experts to eight regions of the country. Please specify from the following regions when ordering your plan:

Region 1: Northeast
Region 2: Mid-Atlantic
Region 3: Deep South
Region 4: Florida & Gulf Coast
Region 5: Midwest
Region 6: Rocky Mountains
Region 7: Southern California & Desert Southwest
Region 8: Northern California & Pacific Northwest

OUR EXCHANGE POLICY

With the exception of reproducible plan orders, we will exchange your entire first order for an equal or greater number of blueprints within our plan collection within **60 days** of the original order. The entire content of your original order must be returned before an exchange will be processed. Please call our customer service department at 1-888-690-1116 for your return authorization number and shipping instructions. If the returned blueprints look used, redlined, or copied, we will not honor your exchange. Fees for exchanging your blueprints are as follows: 20% of the amount of the original order, plus the difference in cost if exchanging for a design in a higher price bracket or less the difference in cost if exchanging for a design in a lower price bracket. (Reproducible blueprints are not exchangeable or refundable.) Please call for current postage and handling prices. Shipping and handling charges are not refundable.

ABOUT REPRODUCIBLES

Reproducibles (often called "vellums") are the most convenient way to order your blueprints. In any building process, you will need multiple copies of your blueprints for your builder, subcontractors, lenders, and the local building department. In addition, you may want or need to make changes to the original design. Such changes should be made only by a licensed architect or engineer. When you purchase reproducibles, you will receive a copyright release letter that allows you to have them altered and copied. You will want to purchase a reproducible plan if you plan to make any changes, whether by using our convenient Customization Program or going to a local architect.

ABOUT REVERSE BLUEPRINTS

Although lettering and dimensions will appear backward, reverses will be a useful aid if you decide to flop the plan. See Price Schedule and Plans Index for pricing.

ARCHITECTURAL AND ENGINEERING SEALS

Some cities and states now require that a licensed architect or engineer review and "seal" a blueprint, or officially approve it, prior to construction. Prior to application for a building permit or the start of actual construction, we strongly advise that you consult your local building official who can tell you if such a review is required.

ABOUT THE DESIGNS

The architects and designers whose work appears in this publication are among America's leading residential designers. Each plan was designed to meet the requirements of a nationally recognized model building code in effect at the time and place the plan was drawn. Because national building codes change from time to time, plans may not fully comply with any such code at the time they are sold to a customer. In addition, building officials may not accept these plans as final construction documents of record as the plans may need to be modified and additional drawings and details added to suit local conditions and requirements. Purchasers should consult a licensed architect or engineer, and their local building official, before starting any construction related to these plans.

LOCAL BUILDING CODES AND ZONING REQUIREMENTS

At the time of creation, these plans are drawn to specifications published by the Building Officials and Code Administrators (BOCA) International, Inc.; the Southern Building Code Congress International, (SBCCI) Inc.; the International Conference of Building Officials (ICBO); or the Council of American Building Officials (CABO). These plans are designed to meet or exceed national building standards. Because of the great differences in geography and climate throughout the United States and Canada, each state, county, and municipality has its own building codes, zone requirements, ordinances, and building regulations. Your plan may need to be modified to comply with local requirements. In addition, you may need to obtain permits or inspections from local governments before and in the course of construction. We authorize the use of the blueprints on the express condition that you consult a local licensed architect or engineer of your choice prior to beginning construction and strictly comply with all local building codes, zoning requirements, and other applicable laws, regulations, ordinances, and requirements. Notice: Plans for homes to be built in Nevada must be redrawn by a Nevada-registered professional. Consult your building official for more information on this subject.

TERMS AND CONDITIONS

These designs are protected under the terms of United States Copyright Law and may not be copied or reproduced in any way, by any means, unless you have purchased reproducibles which clearly indicate your right to copy or reproduce. We authorize the use of your chosen design as an aid in the construction of one single- or multi-family home only. You may not use this design to build a second or multiple dwellings without purchasing another blueprint or blueprints or paying additional design fees.

HOW MANY BLUEPRINTS DO YOU NEED?

Although a four-set building package may satisfy many states, cities, and counties, some plans may require certain changes. For your convenience, we have developed a reproducible plan, which allows you to take advantage of our Customization Program, or to have a local professional modify and make up to 10 copies of your revised plan. As our plans are all copyright protected, with your purchase of the reproducible, we will supply you with a copyright release letter. The number of copies you may need: 1 for owner, 3 for builder, 2 for local building department, and 1-3 sets for your mortgage lender.

DISCLAIMER

The designers we work with have put substantial care and effort into the creation of their blueprints. However, because we cannot provide on-site consultation, supervision, and control over actual construction, and because of the great variance in local building requirements, building practices, and soil, seismic, weather, and other conditions, **WE MAKE NO WARRANTY OF ANY KIND, EXPRESS OR IMPLIED, WITH RESPECT TO THE CONTENT OR USE OF THE BLUEPRINTS, INCLUDING BUT NOT LIMITED TO ANY WARRANTY OF MERCHANTABILITY OR OF FITNESS FOR A PARTICULAR PURPOSE. ITEMS, PRICES, TERMS, AND CONDITIONS ARE SUBJECT TO CHANGE WITHOUT NOTICE.**

IT'S EASY TO ORDER JUST VISIT EPLANS.COM OR CALL TOLL-FREE 1-800-521-6797

OPEN 24 HOURS, 7 DAYS A WEEK
If we receive your order by 3:00 p.m. EST, Monday-Friday, we'll process it and ship within two business days. When ordering by phone, please have your credit card or check information ready.

CANADIAN CUSTOMERS
Order Toll Free 1-877-223-6389

ONLINE ORDERING
Go to: www.eplans.com

After you have received your order, call our customer service experts at 1-888-690-1116 if you have any questions.

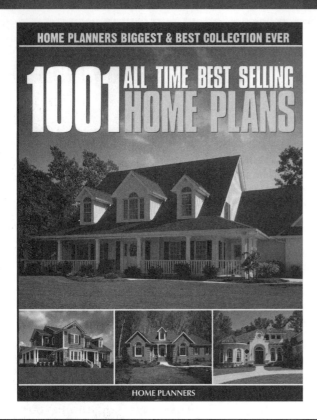
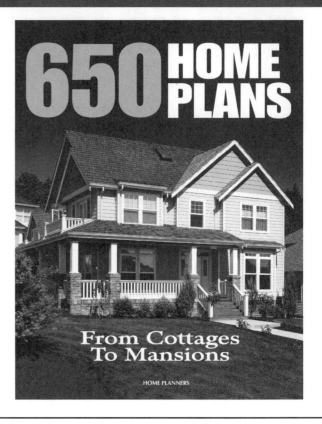
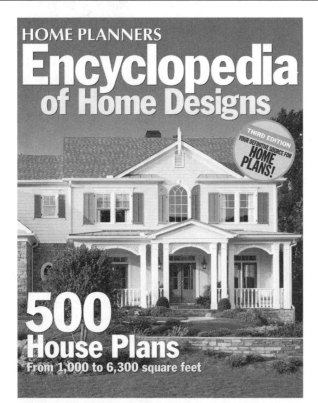

Build Or Remodel Your Dream Home

With HomePlanners Books & Blueprints

Choose Any of These Books— 10% Off the Regular Price

Hanley Wood brings you more choices from leading home plan designers than any other source. Our relationships with leading architects and designers give you access to the best home plans and a more comprehensive selection of home styles.

BOOK SALE!
ALL BOOKS 10% OFF REGULAR PRICE

FINE LIVING
Home Designs with Luxury Amenities
$17.95 NOW ONLY $16.15
ITEM: FL

CONTEMPORARY HOME PLANS
Sleek designs for modern lifestyles
$10.95 NOW ONLY $9.85
ITEM: CM2

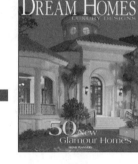

AMERICAN DREAM HOMES
A collection of luxury designs
$19.95 NOW ONLY $17.95
ITEM: SOD2

ESTATE DREAM HOMES
Designs of unsurpassed grandeur
$16.95 NOW ONLY $15.25
ITEM: EDH3

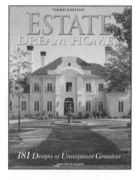

GRAND MANOR HOMES
Premier designs from Country to European
$17.95 NOW ONLY $16.15
ITEM: GMH

LUXURY DREAM HOMES
170 lavish designs
$12.95 NOW ONLY $11.65
ITEM: LD3

VICTORIAN DREAM HOMES
Victorian and Farmhouse plans
$15.95 NOW ONLY $14.35
ITEM: VDH2

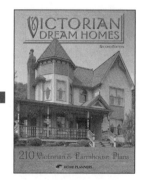

EUROPEAN DREAM HOMES
French, English and Mediterranean designs
$15.95 NOW ONLY $14.35
ITEM: EUR2

OUR BEST PRICES EVER!

hanley▲wood
HomePlanners